CALIFORNIA'S

ARCHITECTURAL FRONTIER

CALIFORNIA'S

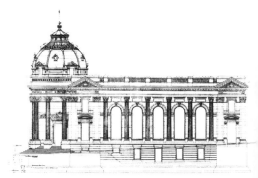

HAROLD KIRKER

ARCHITECTURAL FRONTIER

STYLE AND TRADITION IN THE

NINETEENTH CENTURY

GIBBS M. SMITH, INC.
PEREGRINE SMITH BOOKS
SALT LAKE CITY

Published by Gibbs M. Smith, Inc.
P.O. Box 667, Layton, Utah 84041

Manufactured in the United States of
America

90 89 88 87   5 4 3 2

Third Edition

Book design by J. Scott Knudson

Cover art hand-coloring by ViviAnn Rose,
Logan, Utah

Cover photograph by Chauncey A. Kirk

**Library of Congress Cataloging-in-
Publication Data**

Kirker, Harold.
  California's architectural frontier

  Bibliography: p.
  Includes index.
  1. Architecture—California.
2. Architecture,
Modern—19th century—California.
I. Title.
NA730.C2K5 1986 720'.9794 85-32036
ISBN 0-87905-011-X

FOR MY GRANDMOTHER

CONTENTS

ILLUSTRATIONS

INTRODUCTION

K now that on the right hand of the Indies there is an island called California, very close to the side of the Terrestrial Paradise; . . . the strongest in all the world, with its steep cliffs and rocky shores . . . in the whole island there was no metal but gold." Published in Spain around 1510 by Garcí Ordóñez de Montalvo, the excerpt from the best selling novel *Las Sergas de Esplandian* described California as a place apart, a place akin to paradise — a memorable land with abundant riches. Yet this sixteenth century California was a place in fiction, the name only later appended to a strip of western-most coastal territory in North America.

As time passed, the real California would continue to resemble ever more closely its mythical forebear. California's climate was unsurpassed and did indeed seem to be "very close to the side of the Terrestrial Paradise." Developing a resoundingly strong economy, the state could also boast bulwarks in the realm of intellect and ideas. Its landscape took the breath away, its gold, once stumbled upon, shook loose the settled inhabitants of Eastern America and drew them west. And, for better or worse, California has always been interpreted as a separate place. As Michael Sorkin noted in *California Counterpoint: New West Coast Architecture* (1982), "The whole culture buys the myth that California is adjacent to the U.S., not exactly contiguous with it."

Also from its earliest days of immigrant settlement, first Hispanic and then Anglo, California internalized a dichotomy that would exert a push-pull over its inhabitants and their activities. The place *was* felt to be a land apart, heralded and scorned. But, it was the last frontier, the outermost edge of a more rooted culture. During the nineteenth century California bred radical ideas, yet imbodied them in a conservative materialism; it was, in short, a typical by-product of colonialism. As architectural and social historian Robert Winter has commented in the *Pacific Historical Review* (1961), "The movement of people to the West increased their desire to be like the East, to outdo it perhaps, but to work within its discipline and pattern."

Yet the push of the conservative colonial frontier, not unlike such frontiers reflected in other times and places, was here always beset by a counter pull. California was, and is, as Stanley Tigerman has phrased it in *The California Condition: A Pregnant Architecture* (1983), eternally in a "process of becoming." California as a place of unending process has oftentimes lent a negative aura to the golden land. Impermanence, mobility, pluralism, exploitation: these characteristics, too, are identified with California's process. Joan Didion captures the bite and depression of the California-becoming, ever at odds with its still colonial conservatism, in her many novels and essays of the 1960's, seventies and eighties.

Felt in the region's literature, the instability is echoed in pop culture as well. Written by Don Felder, Don Henley, and Glenn Frey of the Eagles in 1976, "Hotel California" perhaps captures the push-pull most completely:

> On a dark desert highway, cool wind in my hair
> Warm smell of colitas rising up through the air
> Up ahead in the distance, I saw a shimmering light
> My head grew heavy and my sight grew dim
> I had to stop for the night
>
> . . .
>
> Welcome to the Hotel California
> Such a lovely place (such a lovely face)
> Plenty of room at the Hotel California
> Any time of year, you can find it here
>
> . . .
>
> Last thing I remember, I was
> Running for the door
> I had to find the passage back
> To the place I was before
> "Relax," said the night man,
> "We are programmed to receive.
> You can check out any time you like,
> But you can never leave."

Of interest, sensitive California natives—especially those in the arts and humanities—seem to feel the California anxiety the deepest.

A fifth generation California native, Kirker grew up in San Francisco and came of age during the Depression. During the 1930's new buildings were few; Kirker's family, along with others, turned out to view their construction first-hand. The design work of William Wilson Wurster was an especial delight. As an undergraduate collegian at Berkeley, Kirker majored in political science, and transferred to Harvard in 1942. There he began a masters degree in business administration—a degree that was unfinished when he entered the army but resumed following the conclusion of the war. While overseas, European architecture made an impression that overlaid that of the San Francisco and Berkeley buildings of his youth. And it was Europe that determined the historian-to-be's next step: he became an accountant for the War Department, spending the whole of four more years in Italy and Germany. Those years changed the man, and in 1950 Kirker returned to the University of California at Berkeley to study German history. But in one of those quirks of fate, his sought-after mentor had left the college, resulting in the settling of Harold Kirker with imminent American historian Carl Bridenbaugh.

Professor Bridenbaugh was an unusual historian. Not only was he a social historian of Colonial America, he was also an historian who wove architecture into his research—indeed often focusing on it. And in 1950, Bridenbaugh's focus had been keen. His *Cities in the Wilderness; the First Century of Urban Life in America, 1625-1742* had been published in 1938. Throughout the text were references to architecture, architecture as it functioned in its social, economic and cultural context. In 1949, Bridenbaugh wrote *Peter Harrison, First American Architect;* in 1950, *The Colonial Craftsman* and *Seat of Empire; the Political Role of 18th Century Williamsburg.* Indeed, as Charles Hosmer has noted in *Preservation Comes of Age* (1981), Carl Bridenbaugh's *Peter Harrison* was the only book to come out before 1950 that breached the arena of architecture from the vantage of an academic historian, the only pre-1950 study to light upon the preservation issues of contextual archival documentation coupled with the documentation of the surviving buildings themselves.

Initially Harold Kirker had planned to write his dissertation on

Colonial colleges, a topic seemingly in accord with Professor Briden-baugh's own spheres of research. Yet it was Bridenbaugh who suggested that his student write a history of *California* architecture — since there was none to date — placing architects, patrons and buildings firmly in their cultural mileau. By being in the history program at Berkeley, Kirker would have his subject at hand. He would have access to the surviving buildings, and would have a chance to thoroughly review all available archival documentation.

The student would also be embarking upon a study parallel to Bridenbaugh's *Peter Harrison*, a better parallel than the topic of Colonial colleges. Joseph and Peter Harrison had sailed from London to New-port, Rhode Island, in a ship commanded by the elder brother Joseph in 1739. "Lacking gentle birth, inherited lands, or wealth," wrote Bridenbaugh, "they sought to make their way in commerce in the good old eighteenth-century fashion, always trusting that by a turn of fortune they might better themselves and rise in the social scale. That they were on the make, social climbers and fortune hunters if you will, is the key to their careers."

By 1748 Peter, the younger brother, also commanded ships between Britain and the Colonies and was a master of several trades: "ship-handling, navigation, shipbuilding, woodcarving, drafting, cartography, surveying, military engineering and construction, com-merce, and the new agriculture." At this time he was offered the opportunity to design the Redwood Library in Newport (completed in 1750), and followed that design with others of civic type through the year 1760. Harrison was, as Bridenbaugh phrased it, America's first architect. An architect of the first American frontier. An architect in a colonial setting. Now Kirker would evaluate the last continental American frontier — California, particularly Northern California and the San Francisco Bay, as the New England hub of the West. California's setting, too, was colonial. And its architects were largely Peter Harrisons, though of nineteenth century, not eighteenth, century type.

In 1957 Harold Kirker completed *California's Architectural Frontier* as his doctoral dissertation in the American history program at the University of California at Berkeley, although he was then teaching at MIT in Cambridge, where he would remain for the next nine years.

In 1959 he would publish "Eldorado Gothic: Gold Rush Architects and Architecture" in the *California Historical Society Quarterly*. Again in 1959 and in 1960, he would publish short articles in the "American Notes" section of the *Journal of the Society of Architectural Historians* on the Parrott Building (1852) and the Lick House (1861-62), both in San Francisco. (Appropriately, perhaps, Carl Bridenbaugh published an addendum on Peter Harrison — also in the American Notes of the *Journal* in late 1959.) As San Francisco critic Allan Temko had noted in the same periodical in December 1957, and noted with some disgust, no indepth studies of California architecture had yet emerged. To be sure there were several early twentieth century works on the California missions, along with several miscellaneous other studies; and, there were several excellent pre-1950 architectural guidebooks — the Rensches' *The Southern Counties* (1932), *Valley and Sierra Counties* (1933), and *Counties of the Coast Range* (with M.E. Hoover, 1937), consolidated into a single volume, *Historic Spots in California*, in 1948; the WPA Federal Writers' Project for California of 1939; and such State of California publications as the Division of Mines *Mother Lode Country* of 1948.

In addition there were those more purely historical and literary studies that in several noteworthy chapters crossed over into the realm of architecture in its cultural context: Franklin Walker's *San Francisco's Literary Frontier* (1939) and *A Literary History of Southern California* (1950), Glenn S. Dumke's *The Boom of the Eighties in Southern California* (1944), and, most particularly, Carey McWilliams' *Southern California: An Island on the Land* (1946). But a study with California's architectural history as its chief focus did not exist — the closest approximation of such a study was Trent Elwood Sanford's *The Architecture of the Southwest* of 1950, which really treated architecture as "object" and was exemplary for its capture of the feel and spirit of the Southwest, including California. Sanford's role was largely one of critic, and an anti-Victorian critic at that (he described the Carson Mansion in Eureka, California, designed by Joseph and Samuel Newsom in 1885, as a victim of "the Mansard malady and the Victorian virus . . . rising to a full five stories of torture"). Sanford's historical strengths were entirely pre-nineteenth century, while his critical understanding of the region would not again be felt until the middle 1960s and after with the writings of Robert Venturi, Joan Didion, Charles Moore, and John Chase.

In 1960, the Huntington Library published Harold Kirker's dissertation as *California's Architectural Frontier: Style and Tradition in the Nineteenth Century*. As a social and cultural history of California architecture, Kirker's study laid the groundwork for future scholars. Particularly in the 1970's and 1980's, monographs of individual architects first discussed by Kirker began to appear as theses, dissertations and published studies. As a social historian, Harold Kirker was joined by several others — Robert Winter, Thomas Hines, Kevin Starr, John Chase, and the present author. Also in 1960, E. Geoffrey Bangs published *Portals West: A Folio of Late Nineteenth Century Architecture in California* through the California Historical Society. In it, Bangs stated his purpose as stirring the public to see that "anonymous old buildings [with] little or no historical association do have character." *Portals West* predominantly illustrated weathered, deteriorating structures, including residences, schools, churches, firehouses, business blocks, barns and covered bridges. The study was the first signal of California's preservation movement to come, and of an interest in the region's vernacular architecture.

Two more major books on California architecture also made their appearance in 1960: John and Sally Woodbridge's *Buildings of the Bay Area* and Esther McCoy's *Five California Architects*. The Woodbridges' guidebook was the prototype for the hallmark guidebooks of Gebhard and Winter. In 1965 Gebhard and Winter published their first guide to Southern California; in 1977, their second; and in 1985, the first volume of their third. In 1973, Gebhard and Winter, along with the Woodbridges and Robert Montgomery, published a parallel guidebook for the San Francisco Bay Area and Northern California, with a revised edition in 1986; in 1982, the Woodbridges separately published *Architecture — San Francisco: The Guide*. A number of excellent local guidebooks have also followed directly from the original 1960 Woodbridge effort. Esther McCoy's *Five California Architects,* treating the careers of Bernard Maybeck, Irving Gill and R. M. Schindler — with a separate chapter by Randell L. Makinson on Greene and Greene — was first to be entitled *Five California Masterbuilders*. Like all of the 1960 publications, McCoy's had been underway during the late 1950's: the essay on Gill had been published in 1958 as an exhibition catalogue at the Los Angeles County Museum.

As a writer and editor, with a degree in literature from the University of Michigan, McCoy had come to California from New York in 1932. She came for her health and stayed. During the war she worked as an engineering-draftsman for Douglas Aircraft and began her life-long involvement with architecture. In 1945 she entered the office of R. M. Schindler to become an intimate member of the small coterie of Southern California architectural avant-garde. From her first vantage point as editor/writer, Esther McCoy added a second vantage point of astute architectural critic. *Five California Architects* was only the first of many McCoy studies. (She also published a study on Richard Neutra in 1960.) Her fine eye, coupled with her intense skill with a pen, opened many vistas for scholars—vistas into the architectural landscape of twentieth century California. Her 1960 work, like that of Kirker, generated monographs by others during the 1970's and eighties.

In 1962, McCoy added *Modern California Houses* to her body of work. During that same year, Joseph Armstrong Baird, another architectural critic—this time of the nineteenth century—contributed his study on San Francisco architecture: *Time's Wonderous Changes*. (In 1960 he had published "Architectural Legacy of Sacramento: A Study of nineteenth Century Style" in the *California Historical Society Quarterly*.) Unlike each of the other methodological pacesetters of the 1960-63 period, Baird was trained as an art historian and brought to California architectural history a fine connoisseurship, a formalist art historical framework ultimately derived from Heinrich Wölfflin's exegesis on style in *Principles of Art History* (1915; first English translation, 1932), and further refined through such luminaries as Meyer Schapiro and James Ackerman. Baird conceived *Time's Wondrous Changes* as a guide to San Francisco's stylistic development, preparing the study to coincide with the first meeting of the National Trust of Historic Preservation to be held on the West Coast (San Francisco, October 1962). Like the Bangs folio, Baird's work was published by the California Historical Society.

Finally, in 1963 Stephen W. Jacobs would pull together several of the 1960-62 methodologies in his "California Contemporaries of

Frank Lloyd Wright, 1885-1915," presented in *Problems of the Nineteenth and Twentieth Centuries: Studies in Western Art*. In Jacobs was an understanding that social, economic and cultural history, preservation, criticism and formal connoisseurship all contributed in fundamental ways to an intelligent interpretation of California's architecture of the nineteenth and twentieth centuries. Kirker, Bangs, the Woodbridges, McCoy, Baird, and Jacobs together opened a frontier of scholarship.

Yet what followed during the decade of the 1960's remains somewhat peculiar. That decade of social and political unrest, of cultural upheaval, of coming of age, was largely focused on a single island of architectural scholarship. The greatest change for California was the arrival of David Gebhard from the Roswell Museum in Roswell, New Mexico (and previous to that, from graduate studies in Minneapolis). Gebhard has become the most prolific contributor of California architectural studies to date; and it is likely a position that shall remain unchallenged in the years ahead. Beginning in 1963, Professor Gebhard undertook a continuous series of architectural exhibitions (with catalogues) for the Art Gallery at the University of California at Santa Barbara. Architects spotlighted included Joseph and Samuel Newsom, Louis Christian Mullgardt (with Robert Judson Clark), Irving Gill, George Washington Smith, Lloyd Wright, Rudolph Schindler, Kem Weber and Gregory Ain. Southern California, focusing on Los Angeles and Santa Barbara in particular, was also addressed as an urban environment.

By the end of the 1960's, Gebhard was joined as catalogue author by Harriette Von Breton. In 1967, Gebhard published "The Spanish Colonial Revival in Southern California (1895-1930)" in the *Journal of the Society of Architectural Historians*. And, of course, his first guidebook to Southern California (co-authored with Robert Winter) had come out in 1965. David Gebhard followed most closely in the critical wake of Esther McCoy, bringing with him a vibrant interest in late nineteenth and early twentieth century modernism, as well as doctoral training as an art historian. (Prior to California, Gebhard had focused on the work of William Gray Purcell and George Grant Elmslie.) Once on the West Coast, he expanded his interests to include critical analysis of the 1930's, forties, and fifties, with forays extending through the sixties, seventies and eighties.

Outside Santa Barbara, however, the landscape for California architectural studies was strangely dry between 1963 and 1970. In 1968 Roger Olmsted published *Here Today: San Francisco's Architectural Heritage,* with a stylistic analysis and glossary by Joseph Armstrong Baird; Esther McCoy published a book on Southern California modernist Craig Ellwood in the same year. Perhaps, most significantly, several fresh individuals foreshadowed the tenor of the decade ahead. Native Joan Didion began to write on California, often discussing with uncanny acumen the built environment — discussions of the new role of the freeway and the interchange, of the suburban planned tract, and of the shopping center — in *Run River* (1963) and *Slouching Towards Bethlehem* (1968). In 1965, Robert Venturi published extracts from *Complexity and Contradiction in Architecture* in the Yale Architectural Journal *Perspecta* 9-10, while Charles Moore published "You Have to Pay for the Public Life" in the same issue. Both sets of essays, like the writings of Didion, pointed to a terra incognita where an ahistorical understanding of buildings in the West and Southwest would generate a push-pull with the scholarly historicism initiated in the early 1960's.

During this decade, too, Harold Kirker left, and returned to, California scholarship. In 1963, while at MIT, he published a brief note, "The New Theater in Philadelphia of 1791-92," and a more extended article, "Charles Bulfinch: Architect as Administrator," both in the *Journal of the Society of Architectural Historians.* His Bulfinch article paid clear tribute to the socio-cultural methodology of Carl Bridenbaugh. Kirker noted of Bulfinch in his role as Boston chief of police, post-1799, "Bulfinch not only discharged these duties with rectitude but designed the State House in which law was promulgated, the Court House in which it was administered, and the town, county, and state jails in which the guilty were incarcerated. It can also be said he designed many of the buildings and houses, streets and wharves, in which the crimes were committed." In 1964 Professor Kirker published *Bulfinch's Boston* with his twin brother James Kirker, following the book with another Bulfinch study in 1969 entitled *The Architecture of Charles*

Bulfinch. It is perhaps an irony that the second Bulfinch study was written after Harold Kirker returned to California. In January 1966, Kirker settled in at the University of California at Santa Barbara, teaching American culture in the history department. In the same university, albeit in the art department, David Gebhard was also settling in.

The year 1970 opened a satisfyingly full era of traditional California architectural scholarship that extends into our own day. In February 1970 the Institute of American History celebrated 200 years of California history through a conference at Stanford University: featured were nine California historians — John W. Caughey, Walton E. Bean, Rodman Paul, Gerald D. Nash, Don E. Fehrenbacher, Moses Rischin, Earl Pomeroy, Harold Kirker and Andrew Rolle. Kirker's contribution, "California Architecture and its Relation to Contemporary Trends in Europe and America," again stressed that the chief characteristic of California architecture, particularly its earliest architecture, was its colonialism. Several of the conference papers were published in the *California Historical Society Quarterly* in 1972; all of the papers were published as *Essays and Assays: California History Reappraised* in 1973 (the book-length publication was first to be entitled *New Perspectives on California History*).

Yet even as Harold Kirker put forth his thesis — on the surface unchanged from that of the late 1950's — he, too, acknowledged the dichotomy of California as "colonial frontier" and as "place apart." In conclusion he asked: "For example, what are the psychological and social factors which gave the Shingle style its sense of fitness and long ascendency in the San Francisco Bay region? To what extent does the bungalow reflect the mediocrity of life in Southern California, with its desperate perpetuation upon a booming wasteland of the supposedly rural values of a largely midwestern immigration? How faithfully does architecture reveal the extraordinarily exploitive character of California society? Of its pluralism or mobility or impermanence? Is there a correlation between the make-believe character of much of California building in the last half-century and the unreality of contemporary social and political ideas? . . . If . . . the architectural components of this forever-coming-into-being culture has been something of a negative catalogue, that does seem to be the nature of California culture."

Entry into the new decade also served as the watershed for the ahistorical architecture-as-object interpretations that would form their own body of literature in the 1970's and eighties, the very body of interpretations Kirker must also have felt possessed some validity. In 1970, Joan Didion published *Play It As It Lays*. Set in the urban Los Angeles basin and in the desert in and around Las Vegas, the novel hit hard upon those California characteristics of exploitation, aimlessness, and peripatetic mobility. Maria (pronounced Mar-i-ah) Wyeth, the central character, roams the Los Angeles freeways at high speed for whole days at a time in scenes eery with reality, scenes that no one who has driven those freeways could forget. The built environment — freeways, tract houses, shopping centers, stage sets, motels, gambling palaces, trailer parks — is writ large. In 1971, Reyner Banham published *Los Angeles: the Architecture of Four Ecologies,* again commenting on the real-unreal, urban-suburban microcosm of Los Angeles.

Both Didion and Banham (and Venturi and Moore) had been somewhat foreshadowed in their discoveries about Western and Southwestern architecture by Trent Elwood Sanford in 1950. There were basic tenets for the architecture and urban environments of the region that had not been much thought about during the 1950's and 1960's. In the West existed an elemental interplay of space, scale and motion. Space between rural outposts and towns seemed a given, but space between suburbs, between multiple downtowns, between centers, did not. Scale, that sense of vastness of sky and land and water as it related to man-made structures, also began to seem skewed as it became sign (in Las Vegas, in Los Angeles, in West Hollywood). And motion: in the West one must often drive to buildings — whether one cruised along over Route 66 through towns projecting themselves at the highway, or whether one sped around L.A., architecture did become theater, with, as Charles Moore has phrased it, "time controlled viewing." Sanford, in his conservative study of architecture in the Southwest of 1950, had anticipated all of this. After all, a dual existence is fundamental for any work of art — or architecture: buildings are both documents of our past (even our yesterday) and objects in our present. In California the present day objects had taken on a life of their own.

So the 1970's and the first half-decade of the 1980's have been double-edged. Traditional studies of widely differing methodology flourished. As did the counter-culture. Under the umbrella of the former were monographs on R. M. Schindler (Gebhard: 1971, reprinted in 1980; McCoy: *Vienna to Los Angeles,* 1979), Greene and Greene (Makinson: 1974, 1977, 1984; Strand: 1974; W. R. and K. Current: 1974), Bernard Maybeck (Cardwell: 1977; Longstreth: 1983), Julia Morgan (Longstreth: 1977), Willis Polk (Longstreth: 1979; 1983), Richard Neutra (Hines: 1982), Ernest Coxhead (Beach: 1976; Longstreth: 1983), A. C. Schweinfurth (Longstreth: 1983), A. Page Brown (Starr: 1985), Gregory Ain, J. R. Davidson, Raphael Soriano, and Harwell Hamilton Harris (McCoy: 1984), and Charles Moore (Littlejohn: 1984). Two major studies on the Bay Area (or Bay Region) Tradition appeared: Freudenheim's *Building with Nature* of 1974 and *Bay Area Houses* of 1976, edited by Sally Woodbridge.

Exhibition catalogues also contributed to the growing body of work, including not only the Gebhard and Von Breton efforts in Santa Barbara, but in addition catalogues addressing issues of university campus planning, urban development and contemporary architecture. Most recently, two catalogues on architects Myron Hunt (Baxter Art Gallery, California Institute of Technology: 1984) and Hart Wood (Hibbard and Weitze: 1985) have doubled as monographs.

In the field of preservation, studies have appeared in the vein of E. Geoffrey Bangs, illustrating our vanishing heritage. They have also appeared as guides to conservation, law and administration, and as tools for civic decision. In 1978, the Oakland Planning Department published *Rehab Right: How to Rehabilitate Your Oakland House,* a model preservation publication that had effects well outside the East Bay. In 1979, Charles Hall Page (with Michael Corbett as major author) published *Splendid Survivors,* a well-researched documentary analysis of San Francisco's downtown. The year 1980 witnessed the publication of the *Historic American Buildings Survey for California,* with David G. DeLong writing an introduction. And, in 1984, the State of California published the *California Task Force Report,* serving as a kind of summation of the preservation movement in California to date (Roland and Weitze, compilers).

Also within the group of traditional studies were ones treating vernacular architecture and urban design; *California Crazy: Roadside Vernacular Architecture* (Heimann and Georges: 1980), *Cities on Stone* and *Cities of the American West* (Reps: 1976 and 1979), *Exterior Decoration: Hollywood's Inside-out Houses* (Chase: 1982), as well as several on San Francisco and the peninsula (Waldhorn and Olwell: 1976; Pomada and Larsen: 1978; Waldhorn: 1978; Regnery: 1976) and Los Angeles (Gleye: 1981; Moore: 1984). Indices to major historic architectural journals appeared: for *California Architect and Building News*, 1879-1900 (Snyder: 1975) and for *Architect and Engineer of California*, 1905-1928 (Goss: 1982). And finally, in the realm of social history were studies on the California bungalow (Winter: 1974, 1980), West Hollywood (Chase: 1982), the Mission Revival (Weitze: 1984), Benicia (Breugmann: 1980) and Richard Neutra (Hines: 1982). Of course, publications at times crossed over into several catagories, and, of course, shorter journal articles also appeared. Much of the dynamic activity owes itself to the publishing houses of Peregrine Smith and Hennessey & Ingalls. With the publication of the revised edition of Harold Kirker's *California's Architectural Frontier* by Peregrine Smith in 1973, that publisher began to bring out a number of books on California architecture. Hennessey & Ingalls initiated a series on California architecture in 1980. Both publishers remain active today.

But what of the counterpoint publications beginning with Didion's *Play It As It Lays* (1970)? In 1971, Robert Venturi and Denise Scott Brown published "Ugly and Ordinary Architecture, or the Decorated Shed" in *Architectural Forum,* and, in 1972, they published *Learning from Las Vegas* (with Steven Izenour) — the latter previously glimpsed by the same authors as "A Significance for A&P Parking Lots, or Learning from Las Vegas" in *Architectural Forum* of 1968. These irreverent looks at modern architecture — at everyday, low-brow buildings and their surroundings — and, most specifically, at what had become ordinary built space for several prominent cities, suburbs and strips in the West and Southwest, was the proverbial tip of an iceberg. In Southern California, Charles Moore and Charles Jencks would begin commenting on L.A. Moore attempted to illustrate that greater Los Angeles was "really a collection of theme parks," with Walt Disney the civic hero and freeways the local monuments (*The City Observed,* 1984). Jencks wrote about "LA Door," noting its habitat in the sprawling city: Los Angeles and Houston told us "something about the way people like to welcome their guests and show off their edifice to the speeding motorist" (*Daydream Houses of Los Angeles,* 1978). And Didion apotheosized the shopping mall: "They float on the landscape like pyramids to the boom years, all those Plazas and Malls and Esplanades. All those Squares and Fairs. All those Towns and Dales, all those Villages, all those Forests and Parks and Lands . . . They are toy garden cities in which no one lives but everyone consumes, profound equalizers, the perfect fusion of the profit motive and the egalitarian ideal . . . " (*The White Album,* 1979). Not only did people start to think about their recent historic environment ahistorically (with David Gebhard defining a segment of the path through the 1930s and 1940s), but architects began to design ahistorically. In Southern California Charles Moore was joined by an entire group of sympathetic professionals, with perhaps Frank Gehry symbolic of them all. (*California Counterpoint,* 1982; *The California Condition,* 1983.) Los Angeles was a place of many layers, soft at the edges, as Moore had said. California was not only colonial and rooted, but most certainly a place apart.

In 1984 Harold Kirker published "The Role of Hispanic Kinships in Popularizing the Monterey Style in California, 1836-1846" in the *Journal of the Society of Architectural Historians.* In 1987 he will publish *Old Forms On A New Land* as part of a several volume series on California history. In *Old Forms On A New Land* he will look at the typography of stylistic change in California, choosing a single building as representative of each design period. Of course, the present edition of *California's Architectural Frontier* will also become available, in celebration of the twenty-fifth anniversary of the original 1960 publication. Over that quarter of a century our understanding of California's architectural history and its role in the greater West — and in the American culture — has blossomed. That historiography has been enriched by debate, by differences in methodology, and, frequently, by the vibrant personalities of its makers. We are all storytellers, whether our first allegiance is to history, art history, architecture, criticism, or literature — or, even to something else. Probably none of us has it quite right, yet revisionism will pull us toward tomorrow. Professor Kirker has the honor of being one of our first real question-askers. And as American historian Carl Degler has said, without a hard and repeated search for the appropriate questions, there can be no answers.

KAREN J. WEITZE

University of California at Davis
January 1986

PREFACE to the 1960 Edition

I N THE hundred years between the construction of the Franciscan missions and the revival of mission building forms at the end of the nineteenth century, California was an architectural frontier. The distinguishing characteristic of this frontier was colonialism. Although in his germinal essay on the significance of the frontier in American life Frederick Jackson Turner states that the wilderness put the colonist in the log cabin of the Cherokee, in California, on the other hand, the immigrants reproduced the houses they had left behind. The Yurok Indians at the Klamath River, the Russians at Fort Ross, the Spanish-Mexicans on the open country south of Santa Barbara and beside the Sonoma forests, the Americans in the wide valleys of the coast range and on the San Francisco dunes — each in turn built on the California frontier from the memory of old homes and in the manner of old habits.

California's architectural frontier was not limited in time to that brief period following Spanish settlement in 1769, when, to use another of Turner's phrases, the Pacific frontier was the meeting point between savagery and civilization. Nor, as is commonly imagined, did it disappear with the completion of the Pacific railroad in 1869. Architecturally at least, frontier conditions existed in California until the last decade of the nineteenth century, when a group of young designers transformed the imported American Colonial Revival into a native mission movement. Until that time each consecutive wave of colonists brought their past with them and out of it shaped an architecture representative not of conditions on the new frontier but of the older and distant societies from which they emigrated. When this architecture in turn became Californian, reflecting regional rather than alien traditions, the frontier phase was over.

California was a sea frontier upon which a dozen cultures competed and clashed. It was a maritime colony with a professionally varied and cosmopolitan people alien to the economic and social poverty of the Mississippi borders and the Great Plains. In the traditional sense California was not part of the American frontier at all. It was not settled in the westward movement from one undeveloped area to another; it was not a farmer's frontier with an established agrarian society directly behind it to shape the life and character. The China trade and not agriculture opened the Spanish colony to American penetration, and it was to secure the port of San Francisco, not to annex 160,000 square miles of uncharted wilderness, that American troops seized the northern province in the Mexican war. Through this port came not only hundreds of thousands of Argonauts in '49 and '50, but tens of thousands of Chinese in the sixties and seventies. As a sea frontier California attracted a heterogeneous people and produced a society distinguished by cultural diversification.

The extreme isolation of California in the hundred years between Spanish settlement and the completion of the Pacific railroad strengthened the colonists' natural cultural conservatism and accentuated their dependence upon customs brought with them at the time of immigration. In the Spanish-Mexican period sea and overland communications were difficult to maintain because of adverse headwinds along the coast and the hostile nature of the Apache lands; in the period following American annexation in 1846 communications with the United States were equally uncertain because of the long sea voyage around Cape Horn and the several thousand miles of desert and mountain country separating California from the American frontier. As the forty-niners discovered, it was easier to have a shirt laundered in China than to send a letter to Missouri. A decade after the discovery of gold, San Francisco was still twenty-five days by stagecoach from St. Joseph and seventy-five by sail from New York and Boston. And even in the post-Civil War period, when clipper ship and pony express shortened the lines of communication between the Pacific and American frontiers, California was economically and socially more of a colony of the United States than an active partner.

Physical conditions on the California frontier encouraged architectural colonialism by making possible the introduction of every kind of building tradition. Settlement in the last century was principally confined to the coastal region. The moderate and constant climate of this area — the year-round temperature of fifty-eight degrees varies scarcely ten degrees from January to August, and the rainfall, beginning in November and ending in March, averages only ten inches at San Diego and twenty-two at San Francisco — required the colonists to make few compromises with their new environment. The redwood forests extending from San Luis Obispo County north to the Oregon border made it possible for both the Siberian and American frontiersmen to build in their historic wood tradition. On the other hand, the inaccessibility of these groves to the Spanish-Mexicans settled on the southern coastal plains was not an architectural hardship, for the scrub pine, live oak, and Monterey cypress proved adequate to meet their simple need of wood for roof rafters, doorposts, and window lintels.

Even the much-publicized fear of earthquakes proved insignificant as a deterrent to architectural colonialism. For though this fear may have discouraged the use of brick and stone in house construction, these materials were inimical to the California climate and the Spanish-Mexican adobe and American frame building traditions. Except for alterations in some of the plans of the San Francisco churches in the 1850s to include only a rudimentary wooden steeple, or none at all, and a temporary reversion to frame construction in school building after a series of shocks in the late 1860s, the designers of California's public and commercial buildings ignored the menace of earth tremors and constructed their projects in the heavy masonry tradition of Europe and eastern North America.

My purpose in this volume is to explain the colonial nature of California's frontier society in terms of its architecture. To this end I have considered the physical conditions existing on the Pacific frontier, analyzed the character of the California immigration in the frontier period, and examined the economy which produced the most significant building yet raised on any frontier. Finally, I have reconstructed the architecture of nineteenth-century California as a particular study of a unique frontier society. To do this I have invaded two disciplines, without, I hope, seriously violating either. I have accepted architecture as a tool of the social historian. The result is a social history of California architecture. Though noting matters of aesthetic interest, I have concentrated largely on the formation of building standards and tastes in terms of the changing social and economic requirements of a frontier society. Neither a history of California nor a catalogue of buildings, this book will make clear that the social history of architecture is not the direct study of an art but the indirect study of a civilization.

HAROLD KIRKER

Cambridge, Massachusetts
March 1960

CALIFORNIA'S
ARCHITECTURAL FRONTIER

I. THE ADOBE BUILDERS

THE CALIFORNIANS as builders in the frontier period were colonials. Indian, European, and American, each perpetuated on the
Pacific frontier traditional building practices. Though nothing remains
of construction undertaken in California prior to Spanish settlement in
1769, there is evidence that the Yurok Indians of the Klamath River
were the first architectural colonials. Descriptions and photographs of
their redwood lodges show conical-shaped cabins fashioned of boards
crudely split from fallen logs and justify the inference that they were
constructed from the memory of Siberian originals carried to the New
World in migrations of the late ice age. The Yurok lodges were erected
over an excavated circular cellar about four feet in depth and fourteen
in diameter; they had neither posts nor beams but were supported by
grounded planks forming a wall over which a roof of boarding was laid.
Entranceways were painstakingly hacked out of the redwood planks
with flints or elk horns, and the exterior walls were occasionally ornamented with geometric designs suggestive of existing Indian cultures in
Alaska. The Yuroks were able to build in their historic wood tradition
because of the abundance of redwood in the northwestern part of the
state, where they settled some thousand years before the arrival of the
Spanish. As builders they present a striking contrast to the nomadic Indians of the Central Valley and the coastal plains, who, in the absence

I

of cold winters and damp summers, camped on the ground under willow trees, in caves along the riverbanks, or at best in temporary shelters carelessly formed of brush and tule. The Yuroks, in their insistence upon domesticating inherited architectural practices on the California frontier, were not only the first colonials, but they set a pattern hardly deviated from by the consecutive immigrant waves that followed and overwhelmed them.[1]

Neither the European nor American settlers on the California frontier accommodated themselves to the hewed-log dugouts of the Yurok Indians or the brush-and-wattle huts of the coastal aborigines. The improvised shelters hastily thrown up by the Spaniards at their newly founded presidios of San Diego and Monterey, described respectively by their makers as a building of tules and "a chapel of poles and mud," were replaced shortly by the *palizada* lodge, the Spanish variant of the Kentucky log house.[2] This typically frontier-type shelter was constructed of poles set upright in the ground and bound together with leather thongs; it was roofed with earth or thatch and sometimes whitewashed in the interior with lime made from sea shells. Although similar to the kind of structures everywhere erected on the traditional western frontier, the *palizada* lodges were inferior to American models in materials and construction. This inferiority resulted from the lack of suitable building timbers on the southern coastal plains settled by the Spanish and their unfamiliarity with wood construction. And just as the missions were reconstructed in the late eighteenth century in imitation of Franciscan buildings in Mexico and Old Spain, the presidios were rebuilt in traditional adobe brick as soon as conditions permitted the construction of permanent buildings.[3]

[1] William White Howells, *Back of History* (Garden City, N.Y., 1954), p. 280; Albert Louis Kroeber, *Handbook of the Indians of California* (Washington, D.C., 1925), pp. 78-79.

[2] Francisco Palou, *The Founding of the First California Missions*, trans. and arranged by Douglas S. Watson (San Francisco, 1934), p. 109.

[3] G. W. Hendry and J. N. Bowman, "Spanish and Mexican Adobes and Other Buildings in the Nine San Francisco Bay Counties, 1776 to about 1850" (1940), p. 16, MS in the Bancroft Library; Irving Berdine Richman, *California under Spain and Mexico, 1535-1847* (Boston, 1911), p. 332.

It was not the Spanish, nor even the Americans, who brought the art of palisades building to perfection on the California frontier. This distinction belongs to the Russians settled at Fort Ross on the Sonoma coast north of San Francisco. At the time of its construction in 1812, Fort Ross was the center of the Russian fur trade in the Pacific and the most formidable military establishment in California. Its buildings, described in 1841 as "sturdily constructed" of redwood logs "nicely mortised together at the corners," included a two-story barracks, several houses, a chapel, and numerous shops.[4] One of these structures was sketched by the French traveler Eugène Duflot de Mofras prior to destruction in the Mexican period and is reproduced in Plate 2. A particularly fine example of California frontier architecture, it not only demonstrates a degree of carpentry skill altogether exceptional in the Spanish period, but gives authority to the belief that as many as one third of the Russians at Fort Ross were experienced woodworkers and builders.

The single important Russian remain in California is the Greek Orthodox Chapel at Fort Ross. A curious building measuring twenty-five by thirty-two feet and surmounted by a pentagonal-shaped tower that once held some famous bells, it is believed to have been lighted solely by round windows in the shallow dome; the existing fenestration represents changes made during restorations in 1915-1917. Even in its present mutilated state, this military chapel is a fine example of an alien wood culture, which could be reproduced in California because of the exceptional building talents of the colonists and the abundance of redwood along that part of the coast settled by the Russians.[5]

Aside from these early efforts in wood construction on the Pacific frontier, the common building material in the Spanish-Mexican period was adobe. Richard Henry Dana wrote of Monterey in 1835, "The

---

[4] *History of Sonoma County* (San Francisco, 1880), pp. 364-366; Hubert Howe Bancroft, *History of California* (San Francisco, 1884-1890), II, 629, in *The Works of Hubert Howe Bancroft.*

[5] E. O. Essig, "The Russian Settlement at Ross," *California Historical Society Quarterly*, XII (Sept. 1933), 201, hereafter cited as *CHSQ*; Mildred (Brooke) Hoover, *Historic Spots in California: Counties of the Coast Range* (Stanford, 1937), pp. 640-643; William Wilson Wurster, "California Architecture for Living," *California Monthly*, XLIV (Apr. 1954), 19.

houses here, as everywhere else in California, are of one story, built of clay."[6] Alfred Robinson tells of meeting a Yankee carpenter in the same period who lived in what was considered "a novelty in California," a wooden house made with his craft.[7] San Francisco was without a frame structure until 1836; in Los Angeles the adobe tradition went unchallenged until far into the American period. The term "adobe," as used in reference to California's architectural frontier, denotes both the mud building material and the structure itself. In the absence of any important civic or commercial building, it is confined largely to domestic architecture.

The use of adobe is another example of architectural colonialism, for at the time of Spanish colonization in North America the typical farmhouse in both Old and New Spain was constructed either of rubblestone or mud blocks. As has already been noted, California's moderate climate and the availability of familiar adobe materials made it easy for the Spanish-Mexican immigrants to follow traditional architectural practices. And though the colonials preferred black loam as an adobe substance, the weight and fragility of the finished block precluded long hauling, and every kind of local soil was used.

The work of the adobe builders is the subject of greater misunderstanding than any phase of California frontier architecture. For though the rude mud dwellings of the Spanish-Mexicans accurately indicate the primitive level of the society that produced them, the colonial period is widely regarded as an important stage of Andalusian manorial civilization—an era of sunshine and achievement that bequeathed to the materialistic American conquerors all that is best in their culture. To state that this conception, at least in an architectural sense, has no validity is not necessarily to question the sincerity of the late nineteenth-century romanticists. Whatever the historical truth regarding provincial culture in California, the regional writers fashioned their product from a past as substantial as that drawn upon in the concurrent idealization of the Pilgrim Fathers, or that even more successful manufacture, the chivalric

[6] *Two Years before the Mast* (New York, 1841), pp. 100-101.
[7] *Life in California* (New York, 1846), p. 110.

Old South. Nevertheless, because architecture is considered here primarily for what it tells about the frontier society that produced it, the major part of this chapter is concerned with a critical examination of myth and reality in Spanish-Mexican secular building.

Before considering the long-surviving legend of a Spanish manorial architecture in California, something must be said regarding Franciscan construction on the Pacific frontier. It is true that the Franciscan missions have been the subject of exhaustive literary treatment; it is also true that for all this body of literature the buildings are significant only in a limited regional sense and can scarcely be compared to contemporary examples in the Southwest, or even to earlier models in Mexico. Nonetheless, Franciscan building deserves mention in this study both as the source for the mission movement, which ended the frontier phase of California architecture in the last decade of the nineteenth century, and as an outstanding example of cultural colonialism.

Despite the statement of Father Englehardt that the Franciscan builders drew their architectural inspiration directly from the land, every feature of the so-called California mission style owes its origin to Mexican models. The elaborate Churrigueresque tradition common to contemporary Mexican and southwestern church architecture was not imitated on the West Coast because of a lack of professional architectural knowledge and the extreme primitiveness of Indian building skills. Instead, the California missions were constructed along the simple, rugged lines of the earliest Franciscan buildings in the New World, such as the cathedral and chapel of San Francisco at Cuernavaca.

Though the pioneer mission San Diego de Alcalá was founded by Father Junípero Serra in 1769, it was not until twenty years later that the California mission style came into being. The domestication of Franciscan architectural forms in California was the work of Father Fermín de Lasuén, who was born in Old Spain and labored in Mexico and Lower California prior to succeeding to the nine "unpretentious thatch-covered structures" left at the time of Serra's death in 1784. Lasuén was a true colonial in trying to reconstruct in California the world that he had formerly known, and with the aid of fellow missionaries, a handful of ar-

tisans, and a small body of semiskilled Indian laborers he rebuilt the missions in adobe, stone, and tile after familiar Franciscan models.

The construction of the missions was left to the padres themselves.
Santa Clara was the work of a Franciscan who built extensively for Father Serra in Mexico; San Luis Rey was designed by the priest Antonio
Peyrí of Catalonia. Father Antonio Ripoll, the most skilled of the Franciscan builders, reconstructed the façade of the mission church at Santa
Barbara from a plate in a Spanish edition of Vitruvius, and José María
de Zalvidea designed the surviving El Molino Viejo (The Old Mill)
at the present site of San Marino from Mexican models. Indian neo-
phytes supplied most of the labor in the building of the missions, and
though skilled masons are known to have worked at Capistrano and San
Luis Rey, the Franciscan fathers were only occasionally assisted by
craftsmen from the presidios or artisans contracted in Mexico for short
periods.

The Franciscan builders deviated from Mexican models only when
forced to by the poverty of native skills; and, excepting a simplification
in tile construction, and possibly the widening of roof eaves to protect
adobe walls from water erosion, they introduced no new elements into
California architecture. Whenever possible the mission builders used
stone or kiln-burned brick in the construction of the massive piers supporting roof and arcade and in strengthening door and window openings. In many instances, however, the walls were constructed of adobe
blocks and merely surfaced with brick masonry. The thatched roofs so
characteristic of the eighteenth-century missions were gradually replaced
with tile in order to lessen the danger of Indian attack with burning ar-
rows. The mission tiles, crudely fashioned on tapering wood molds and
burned in primitive kilns, were simpler and somewhat larger than the
Spanish model from which they were copied. These changes were necessary because of the lack of building skills and, legend notwithstanding,
were not the result of shaping over the thighs of Indian maidens.

For all of their religious significance and romantic connotations, the
Franciscan missions are of only limited importance to a social history of
California architecture. With the secularization of the Franciscan prop-
erties in 1833, the missions fell into picturesque ruin (Plate 1), and

they continued isolated and forgotten until the last decade of the nineteenth century, when they were discovered as a native source for the
Colonial Revival which swept the nation following the Philadelphia
Centennial Exposition. They had no effect whatsoever upon the secular
architecture of presidio, pueblo, or rancho. And it is these establishments
—primitive and poor though they were—to which one must turn for an
understanding of the life and architecture of California in the several
troubled decades preceding American annexation in 1846.

It was said earlier that the work of the adobe builders is the subject of
greater misunderstanding than any phase of California frontier architecture. This is largely the result of the uncertain state of Spanish-Mexican
mud-block building at the time when the Colonial Revivalists "discovered" the so-called Andalusian architecture. For by the last decade of the
nineteenth century most of the adobes of the former presidios and pueblos had either disappeared or were in radically altered condition. Hence,
the western romanticists had far greater freedom in their dedicated task
of fabricating the legend of Spanish California than was enjoyed by
either the New England or southern mythmakers.

The architectural legend of Spanish California was given classic statement in Helen Hunt Jackson's novel *Ramona*, where "the representative house of the half barbaric, half elegant, wholly generous and free-
handed life . . . under the rule of the Spanish and Mexican viceroys" is
pictured as a pastel-tinted hacienda with tile roofs, carved woodwork,
cantilevered balconies, and glazed galleries opening onto brick-paved
verandas and walled gardens.[8] This doubtful picture is based upon un-
reliable contemporary testimony and an inaccurate interpretation of the
much-reconstructed remains of several extant adobes. Typical of the
former is the description left by Horace Bell of "all of the old Spanish
houses . . . of the good old times" as freshly whitewashed manors with
pine-planked floors and columned verandas.[9] The validity of such
sources can be judged by the fact that when Spanish rule ended in 1822
there was apparently only one planked floor in the entire province, and
that was in the governor's house at Monterey. The columns, fanlighted

[8] Boston, 1884, p. 16.
[9] *Reminiscences of a Ranger* (Santa Barbara, 1927), p. 198.

doorways, small-paned windows, brick chimneys, and balconies that Bell and the later romanticists found so endearing are not representative of the Spanish period at all but were introduced into California by New England merchants and belong only to the decade immediately preceding American annexation.

Not only do most of the surviving Spanish Colonial houses represent Yankee rather than Mediterranean architectural traditions, but many of them were constructed long after the Spanish period ended. The land for the famous Rancho Camulos, twenty-five miles east of Mission San Buenaventura and credited by Rexford Newcomb as the home of Ramona, was not granted until 1839, and, according to one authority, its oldest existing building dates from 1853.[10] The celebrated Casa Estudillo on the Plaza at San Diego, better known as "Ramona's Marriage Place," was not begun until at least three years after California became a Mexican province; its present form is largely the result of questionable reconstruction undertaken in 1910.[11] Even the well-known Casa de la Guerra at Santa Barbara, so often cited as a representative Spanish dwelling, postdates the Mexican revolution. Construction on this house was begun possibly as early as 1819, but the date 1826, stamped upon an adobe brick in the structure, more accurately places it within the Mexican period.[12] It is significant that the dwelling house on the Rancho Guájome in San Diego County, where Helen Hunt Jackson stayed as a guest while gathering material for her novel, was built by an American immigrant in 1852-1853 from money earned in supplying beef to the forty-niners.

Despite the certainty that less than twenty private land grants were patented in the entire half century of Spanish rule and that the Mexican government continued this conservative land policy for at least another decade, legend has made the rancho the center of Spanish Colonial

[10] Rexford Newcomb, *The Old Mission Churches and Historic Houses of California* (Philadelphia, 1925), p. 345; Eva Scott Fényes and Isabel López de Fáges, *Thirty-Two Adobe Houses of Old California* (Los Angeles, 1950), p. 52.

[11] Trent Elwood Sanford, *The Architecture of the Southwest* (New York, 1950), pp. 237-238.

[12] Fényes and De Fáges, p. 58.

building in California. Until secularization of the mission lands in 1833, however, provincial society was confined almost entirely to seven military and civil establishments planted in the late eighteenth century from San Diego north to San Francisco. The military stations, called presidios, were typically fortified areas about one hundred yards square, and each included a church, officer and troop quarters, various warehouses, and a jumble of adobe and thatched cottages. The free towns, or pueblos, comprised four square leagues divided among the colonists as house sites, orchard and garden tracts, and communal pasturage. As the historic Spanish town plan proved adaptable to the flat, open coastal areas, the pueblos were laid out in the traditional gridiron scheme of parallel land holdings grouped about a plaza or common.

Excepting the capital of Monterey, the presidios were miserable establishments, badly planned, poorly constructed, and indifferently garrisoned. The English navigator Beechey reported San Francisco in 1826 to be a desolate enclosure of mud huts; Santa Barbara was described three years later as consisting of a few hundred poor houses constructed of clay, tule, and tile.[13] Edwin Bryant, who visited the military centers immediately after Mexican capitulation in 1846, pictured them as hardly more than heaps of mud, without the "smallest pretensions to architectural taste or beauty."[14] An early nineteenth-century description of the buildings of San Jose as "miserable shacks with palisaded walls and sod roofs" suggests that the pueblo shelters were indistinguishable from those of the presidio.[15] The lost colony of Branciforte had only five settlers and seven huts "badly roofed with tule" at the time of Mexican independence; Los Angeles at least survived—if only as a poor, treeless settlement of single-story, flat-roofed adobes huddled about a slumbering plaza.[16]

[13] Bancroft, *History of California*, II, 588; Robinson, *Life in California*, p. 41.

[14] *What I Saw in California* (New York, 1848), p. 316.

[15] Katharine Coman, *Economic Beginnings of the Far West* (New York, 1912), II, 138.

[16] Bancroft, *History of California*, II, 156, 626; J. Gregg Layne, "Annals of Los Angeles," Part I, *CHSQ*, XIII (Sept. 1934), 203-204; idem, "The First Census of the Los Angeles District," Historical Society of Southern California, *The Quarter-*

Not only is the age of the rancho largely limited to the decade immediately preceding annexation, but there was nothing about the rancho itself to suggest the European manor to which, in fiction at least, it is so often compared. For whatever the wealth of the rancher in land and cattle, his adobe dwelling differed hardly at all from the rude shelters of presidio and pueblo. Though there is one authentic picture of a ranch house in the San Gabriel Valley with adobe wings enclosing a patio in which a fountain stirred in the shade of pepper trees, contemporary descriptions picture the colonial dwellings as cottages of unburnt brick without proper floors, chimneys, doors, or windows.[17] The "altogether typical" ranch house of Juan José Domínguez, whose 75,000 acres made him one of the greatest landowners in California, was a poor structure with an earthen floor and a tar roof.[18] In 1831 Alfred Robinson described the dwelling of a large ranch near San Juan Bautista as a hut constructed of sticks plastered with mud; as late as 1849 Alonzo Delano pictured the Spanish-Mexican ranchers living in "rude houses without floors, built of sun-dried brick."[19] The Indian peons lived apart from the rancheria in quarters only slightly less primitive than those of the landowner. They were smaller, however, had thinner adobe walls, and, if possible, contained even less household furnishings.

The secular architecture of Spanish California was of primitive mud-block construction. Testimony to this fact by such trustworthy travelers as Richard Henry Dana and Alfred Robinson has already been noted. It has also been observed that, though the adobe builders preferred black loam for their building projects, every kind of local soil was utilized. The three-foot-deep walls of the typical one-room shelter of the Spanish-Mexicans required about one thousand mud blocks, and these were

---

ly, XVIII (Sept.-Dec. 1936), 81-99. The magazine of the Historical Society has been known variously as *Publications*, *Annual Publications*, and *The Quarterly*. Hereafter references to these periodicals will be cited as *HSSCQ*.

[17] Susanna (Bryant) Dakin, *A Scotch Paisano* (Berkeley, 1939), p. 28; Theodore Henry Hittell, *History of California*, I (San Francisco, 1885), 413.

[18] Robert Glass Cleland, *The Cattle on a Thousand Hills* (San Marino, 1951), p. 9.

[19] Robinson, p. 111; Alonzo Delano, *California Correspondence*, ed. Irving McKee (Sacramento, 1952), p. 27.

shaped in a rude mold to an average size of sixteen inches in width and twenty in length; they were generally three to six inches thick and weighed from twenty to forty pounds. Straw was preferred as binding for the adobe substance, but inferior strengtheners such as shells, sticks, birds' nests, tule, and even refuse were frequently resorted to.

Because wood was used only in the support of the cottage roof, and in strengthening the several openings in the mud-block walls, the scarcity of timber along the coast south of Santa Barbara and about the cove of Yerba Buena was not a hardship to the Spanish-Mexican builders. The use of wood for flooring was practically unknown before 1835; the earth on the site, tamped to a degree of smoothness and occasionally hardened by watering, served as the adobe floor. Doors and windows were protected against the intrusion of weather and animals by rawhide fastenings hung across the openings or stretched on a frame of poles and set against casements and door frames.

Glass was rarely available before the last decade of Mexican rule, and its use was limited to the dwellings of foreigners or wealthy natives. In 1832 Hugo Reid noted with great surprise the fact that a settler in Los Angeles, a Kentucky silversmith, had placed glass in his grated windows.[20] The second-story glazed gallery of the so-called Glass House, or Casa Materna of the Vallejo family, overlooking the Pajaro Valley in Monterey County and supposedly erected in 1824, is sometimes cited as an example of provincial glasswork. As there were no two-story houses in Monterey before 1835, this so-called Spanish glazing must be considered a fiction. In the outlying regions of the provincial capital there were apparently no glazed windows before William Hartnell erected his adobe on the Rancho Alisal in 1835. That same year Dana noted that some of the wealthy *Monterreyanos* used glass, but his general conclusion was that the windows of the California adobe dwellings were unglazed openings occasionally made secure by setting wooden poles or iron bars a few inches apart in the casement.[21]

[20] Dakin, *Scotch Paisano*, p. 9.

[21] James Miller Guinn, *History and Biographical Record of Monterey and San Benito Counties* (Los Angeles, 1910), I, 266; Dakin, *The Lives of William Hartnell* (Stanford, 1949), p. 181.

In romance the houses of the colonial period are invariably roofed with red Spanish tiles. However, the early discovery of the La Brea pits in the Cahuenga Valley of Los Angeles, and the subsequent uncovering of similar deposits in Santa Barbara, Santa Clara, San Luis Obispo, and San Diego, made asphalt the common roofing material in colonial California. Excepting some rude shakes manufactured by George Yount and Charles Brown for General Mariano Guadalupe Vallejo in 1833, the use of shingles in roofing was unknown until Thomas Larkin introduced them at Monterey several years later. In the Spanish-Mexican period the tar quarries were communally owned and, according to an account of the La Brea pits left by a Kentucky mountain man in 1828, the production of roofing material was the major industry of the pueblo of Los Angeles.[22]

The low cost of extraction and the ease of installation explain the favor asphalt achieved in a climate permitting the use of the flat roof. Because this kind of construction was unfamiliar to the culturally conservative American immigrants, its general acceptance was delayed until a second generation of Californians had shaken off inherited building traditions. Nonetheless, in 1854 the *California Farmer* advised its readers to roof their houses with tar and gravel as had the Angelenos of half a century before; and a year later an advertisement in the *Alta California* proclaimed Santa Barbara asphalt unrivaled as a material for house foundations, roofs, and street paving.[23]

The assertion that the first fireplace in California was built into the Munrás Adobe at Monterey in 1822 is highly improbable, for it was not until thirteen years later that George Yount and Thomas Larkin introduced this feature into domestic architecture. The Spanish-Mexicans cooked their food entirely out of doors and warmed their houses by a pan of coals set upon the floor. Even after the interior fireplace was made part of the Monterey Colonial culture, it was extremely uncommon out-

[22] "The Chronicles of George C. Yount," ed. Charles L. Camp, *CHSQ*, II (Apr. 1923), 53; Guinn, "Los Angeles in the Adobe Age," *HSSCQ*, IV (1897), 51-52.

[23] *The California Farmer and Journal of Useful Sciences*, Mar. 2, 1854, p. 69; *Alta California*, Dec. 1, 1855.

side of the provincial capital. San Jose is reported to have been without a single chimney in 1841; five years later not one Spanish or Mexican house in San Francisco was fitted with a fireplace.[24] The reluctance of the Mexicans to use interior fires is evident from a 1928 report which revealed that not one third of sixty-five adobes in Los Angeles County had fireplaces.[25] It is clear that the simplicity of provincial cooking, the mildness of the climate, and a primitive building knowledge added environmental sanctions to an inherited Spanish prejudice against interior fires.

Excepting the barracks of hewn redwood logs erected at Fort Ross in 1812, there was not a single two-story house in all California before Thomas Larkin began his building operations in Monterey in 1835. The belief that William Hartnell opened his school, El Seminario de San José, on the Rancho Alisal near Salinas in a two-story adobe building in 1834 has been corrected by his biographer; reference to the huge adobe of Don Bernardo Yorba in the Santa Ana River canyon as a two-story dwelling is an example of the many exaggerations regarding this lost house.[26] The Monterey Customhouse, one of the few existing buildings to span the Spanish, Mexican, and American periods, dates from 1814; it was rebuilt, however, in 1841-1842 by Larkin, and the second-story addition to the north wing and the portico on the ocean side are the results of this reconstruction. Several other two-story Monterey adobes, such as the Casa Amesti and the Cooper House, dating in part from the early years of Mexican independence, positively owe their present height to a later period of New England architectural supremacy. The dormer window of the Gaspar Oreña Adobe at Santa Barbara, to which a regional writer has drawn attention in an undocumented study including several two-story Spanish Colonial houses, is certainly

[24] Federal Writers' Project, "Adobes and Old Buildings in Monterey" (1937), p. 121, MS in the Bancroft Library; T. H. Hittell, *California*, I, 413; Bryant, *What I Saw in California*, p. 324.

[25] Marion Parks, "In Pursuit of Vanished Days," HSSCQ, XIV (1928), 13.

[26] Hoover, *Counties of the Coast Range*, p. 233; Dakin, *Hartnell*, p. 181; Helen Smith Giffen, "Some Two-Story Adobe Houses of Old California," HSSCQ, XX (Mar. 1938), 7.

not representative of the adobe age and probably dates from a twentieth-century restoration.[27]

The general absence of mention of staircases and balconies in the detailed descriptions of pre-Larkin adobes supports the assumption that building timbers sufficiently strong to carry the weight of a second story were not generally available to house builders prior to American lumbering operations in the early forties. The reference to a "balcony" on the commandant's house at Santa Barbara in Duhaut-Cilly's description of 1827-1828 must be an error, as earlier in his account of California the French traveler characterized every structure at both the presidios of Santa Barbara and Monterey as single-story buildings.[28] These observations were made two years after the balcony-bearing Casa Amesti in Monterey is said to have been constructed. James McKinley, a Scottish seaman, married Carmen Amesti and lived in the family adobe after 1848; and presumably it was he who added the second story, the balcony, the brick fireplace, and such other features that Thomas Larkin's example had established as the Monterey vernacular architecture. The latticework balcony of the Juan Bandini Adobe on the Plaza at San Diego is not part of the original structure but represents an addition made at the time the house was converted into a hotel in 1860.[29]

At this point the typical dwelling of "the half barbaric, half elegant, wholly generous and free-handed life . . . under the rule of Spanish and Mexican viceroys" has been reduced from a storied manor house to a one-room cottage with a dirt floor and a tar roof. Nor was the bleak aspect of the provincial dwelling softened by the tree-shaded gardens so dear to the late nineteenth-century romanticists. "It is a peculiarity of the Mexicans," reported a foreign traveler in 1846, "that they allow no shade or ornamental trees to grow near their houses."[30] This observation

[27] Clarence C. Cullimore, *Santa Barbara Adobes* (Santa Barbara?, 1948), pp. 124-125.

[28] "Duhaut-Cilly's Account of California in the Years 1827-28," trans. Charles Franklin Carter, *CHSQ*, VIII (June 1929), 157.

[29] Writers' Program, *Monterey Peninsula* (Stanford, 1941), p. 82; "Adobes and Old Buildings," pp. 14-16; Giffen, *Casas & Courtyards: Historic Adobe Houses of California* (Oakland, 1955), pp. 19-20.

[30] Bryant, p. 385.

suggests that the controlling factors in the selection and development of building sites were safety, water, and sunlight. The Californian constructed his adobe on elevated ground to protect the mud walls from water erosion; the house was placed upon an open, treeless site to insure continuous sunlight and to guard against Indian attack and stock thieving.

The extreme simplicity of the adobe shelter has been imputed to an inherited Spanish tradition of austerity. In matters of general design and materials this is unquestionably true. However, subsequent emulation of American architectural novelties by the Spanish and Mexican provincials in the relatively prosperous decade prior to annexation supports the conclusion that the poverty of their houses, as distinct from their style, was the result of a lack of building knowledge, talent, and tools. The California pastoralist was his own architect and master builder; he had neither the skills nor the means for architectural refinements. Indeed, almost the only ornamentation in colonial building resulted from the vulnerability of adobe bricks to rain and flood. For though the poorer shelters rested directly upon the soil and were sometimes eroded away by ground water, whenever possible the adobe was raised upon small rock foundations and the roof was extended out from the wall in a wide eave. These protective devices were occasionally given definite architectural treatment as in the design of foundation rockwork, in the selection of curious stones for a doorstep or gatepost, and more rarely, in the form of a covered corridor.

The disparity between the realities of provincial architecture and the myth of a splendid Andalusian manorial building tradition is too obvious to require further comment. The question remains as to the origin of the myth. Given the insubstantial nature of adobe construction, it could be assumed that in time both the dwellings of provincial California and all evidence of their lowly nature disappeared. But even if this is largely true of urban adobe construction, there survived far into the present century a number of houses, such as the Casa de Soto at Monterey (Plate 3), which—though scorned alike by writers of romantic fiction and of local histories—retain their authenticity as archetypal dwellings of Cali-

fornia's colonial past.[31] Because the Casa de Soto could under no circumstances be accepted as representative of the kind of civilization that
the mythmakers conceived as peculiarly Californian, and such doubtful
"Spanish" houses as the Casa Estudillo at San Diego and the Casa de
la Guerra at Santa Barbara were either in ruinous or radically altered
condition, it was inevitable that the so-called Monterey Colonial houses
would be seized upon as the characteristic dwellings of the Spanish past.
These two-story houses with broad verandas and balconies, brick chimneys, fanlighted doorways, and small-paned windows did indeed represent a colonial tradition; further, many of them were on land with Spanish names or were associated in one way or another with local families.
Without critical investigation, or more likely without the ability to distinguish reality from myth, the romantics took the Monterey Colonial
house as the principal architectural setting for the manorial civilization
that they were busily creating.

In reality Monterey Colonial houses date only from the last years of
the provincial period and, excepting the use of adobe in the construction
of their exterior walls, represent little that is either Spanish or Mexican.
Instead they testify to the increasing American dominance in the economic and cultural life of the colony that resulted from the extension of
the China trade to the Pacific Coast in the years immediately following
the American Revolution. This commerce in otter skins, cowhides, tallow, and Yankee manufactures provided California with its principal
economic activity and induced its first proper secular architecture. Far
from representing the pastoral life of the rancho, the Monterey Colonial
house marks the first important victory in the inevitable struggle between
the mutually antagonistic Spanish-Mexican and American cultures. It is
especially ironic, therefore, that the most visible manifestation of Yankee
superiority should serve as an architectural symbol of the society that it
supplanted.

The work of the adobe builders in the first three and one-half decades
of the nineteenth century stands in direct relationship to their lack of
building skills and the pastoral nature of their society. By 1835, how-

---

[31] Writers' Program, *Monterey Peninsula*, p. 85.

ever, there were in Monterey at least twenty Americans who had profes-
sions associated with or useful to the building trades, and they sought to
satisfy their instinctive cultural conservatism by reproducing in California the houses they left behind in the northeastern United States. But
though the Americans possessed the skills, means, and most of the materials required for the practice of traditional building habits, the necessity to substitute, in part, adobe for wood construction resulted in the
creation of a style known as the Monterey Colonial. This was the work
of the Bostonian Thomas O. Larkin, who opened the first retail store in
the colony, fathered the first American child, and more significant to this
study exerted a greater influence on California secular architecture in the
first half of the nineteenth century than any other single individual.

It is usually thought that Larkin began construction on his widely
imitated house in 1834 (Plate 4). A study of his meticulously kept day-
books, however, establishes the fact that the land for the project was
purchased in April 1835, the foundation laid that same month, and the
structure completed in 1837.[32] The floor plan of the Larkin House followed the American Colonial precedent of two rooms opening off either
side of a central passageway; the construction consisted of a redwood
frame supporting a second story, a broad double veranda, an interior
staircase, and a hipped roof covered with shingles. The house was
equipped with a finished fireplace, interior wallpapering, milled doors,
and windows of American double-sash design. With the several exceptions already noted, every one of these elements was introduced into
California by Thomas Larkin; and, romantic legend notwithstanding,
secular architecture on the Pacific frontier began with the domestication
of New England building standards at Monterey by an American merchant.

Larkin was only following traditional colonial practices in using
familiar Massachusetts models in the design of his Monterey house.
The importance of this structure in the creation of an architectural style
lies in the imagination and freedom with which he adapted eastern building forms to immediate material requirements. Larkin's utilization of

[32] Robert J. Parker, "Building the Larkin House," *CHSQ*, XVI (Dec. 1937),
322-324.

adobe was not, of course, an expression of preference for an indigenous building material; it was rather a reluctant concession to a temporary limitation of labor and equipment that prevented the milling of a sufficient quantity of available redwood for the construction of a completely timbered house. And though he depended upon adobe in the construction of exterior walls, Larkin's introduction of a timber frame to support the weight of an upper story permitted a lighter shell of clay blocks and greater freedom in fenestration than was usual in provincial houses. This acceptance of adobe as a basic building material by the Americans at Monterey, and the subsequent adaptation to New England architectural features by a number of influential Spanish-Mexicans, is a unique instance in California of an important compromise between competing colonial cultures.

Shortly after the completion of the Larkin House the weathering problem of exterior adobe surfaces was solved by covering the mud bricks with clapboards or shingles, which became available as the result of the mechanization of lumbering operations in the Santa Cruz redwood groves in the early 1840's. Larkin, not yet prepared for such extensive use of boarding, conceived the double veranda as a means of protecting his two-story walls from water erosion. It is possible that his ten years' residence in North Carolina acquainted him with the advantages of the double veranda, which was a common feature in the rural architecture of the Old South. Or, more originally, Larkin may have simply extended upward the traditional porch of his boyhood home in Massachusetts.

Alteration, reconstruction, and lack of documentation are common characteristics of the surviving examples of the Monterey Colonial house. But despite their very considerable architectural mutilation, the extant two-story adobe buildings of California testify to the authority of the Larkin House as an architectural prototype. As Plates 4, 5, and 6 demonstrate, the most prominent feature of the style is its horizontal mass, achieved by a low, sloping roof, a long double veranda or, rarely, a cantilevered balcony. The mud-block construction of the Monterey Colonial house is strikingly seen in the much-altered Castro Adobe, where the original plaster, lined in imitation stonework, has fallen away to expose the rough clay bricks (Plate 6). The representative houses all have shingled roofs, though at some date the cedar shakes of the Castro Adobe were overlaid with tile.

Everything about the Monterey Colonial house testifies to its New England origin. The formal fenestration of the Larkin House and the street fronts of the Old Whaling Station and the Cooper House are outstanding examples in Monterey of the symmetrical American Colonial façade. Although it is not possible to know how many of the builders of Monterey-type houses adhered to the traditional floor plan of the Larkin House, the arrangement of two rooms on either side of a central passageway was probably used in the house built by General John Bidwell at the present site of Chico and in the Captain Stephen Smith Adobe erected near Bodega Bay in 1843.[33] The windows of the Monterey Colonial houses were of double-sash design and usually divided into twelve panes, though sometimes twenty-four sections were favored, or even forty-eight, as in the example of the Monterey Whaling Station. Exterior doors, evidently the work of ship carpenters, were paneled and occasionally lighted by an overhead glass fan, such as in the particularly fine Cooper House at Monterey. The addition of glass frames on either side of the entrance door, an architectural distinction of the Castro Adobe, was rare. Such authentic New England elements as the wood-frame lean-tos attached to the Cordero House at Santa Barbara and the Old Whaling Station at Monterey, the board-and-batten construction of the Stokes House at Monterey and the Thomas Hosmer Adobe at Santa Barbara, and the mantelpieces in the Larkin and Vallejo adobes became commonplaces of California architecture after 1840.

As has been suggested, the Monterey Colonial house is a unique California example of compromise between alien immigrant groups. For not only did Larkin adapt to adobe construction, but a number of provincial families built or rebuilt in the new style. The first to copy Larkin's house were of course his neighbors, including Governor Juan Alvarado, whose New England-style adobe is thought to be the second

---

[33] Hoover, *Counties of the Coast Range*, pp. 662-663.

two-story private house in California. In a rush the Spanish-Mexican families of Pacheco, Abrego, Soberanes, and Amesti began construction or reconstruction of houses in the style now known as Monterey Colonial. So industrious were their efforts that the dwellings of the little capital were described in 1842 by a foreign visitor as "prettily-built timber houses with . . . shingled roofs."[34]

But outside of Monterey the Spanish-Mexicans proved stubborn colonials, and, with perhaps a dozen notable exceptions, they refused to accept the architectural compromise effected by the New Englanders and their Spanish-blooded relatives and business associates. In Santa Barbara, for example, Bryant noted only three or four "Americanized" dwellings with "pretensions to tasteful architecture, and comfortable and convenient interior arrangement."[35] Outstanding among these was the adobe of Alpheus B. Thompson, a Yankee merchant married to Francisca Carrillo and possessor of the finest house in Santa Barbara. Thompson's adobe, a two-story building with a shingled roof, was apparently very difficult to finish, for the builder wrote to his colleague Abel Stearns in Los Angeles that he would "rather undertake to build a line of Battleships in the U.S. than a house in Calif."[36]

The construction of a Monterey-type house presented the Angelenos with even more formidable obstacles, and as late as 1852 there were only three two-story dwellings in the southern pueblo and its vicinity. One of these was the house Hugo Reid constructed in 1838 of heavy beams brought from the San Bernardino mountains and clapboard wall-sheathing milled near the site.[37] Another, the Lugo Adobe, erected on the Plaza about 1840 with a traditional flat asphalt roof, may have been, with the exception of Los Cerritos, the only two-story, brea-roofed structure in provincial California. Los Cerritos, built about 1844 near

[34] Reuben Lukens Underhill, *From Cowhides to Golden Fleece* (Stanford, 1939), p. 53; "Edward Vischer's First Visit to California," trans. and ed. Erwin G. Gudde, *CHSQ*, XIX (Sept. 1940), 196.

[35] Page 384.

[36] Giffen, "Two-Story Adobe," p. 13; *China Trade Days in California: Selected Letters from the Thompson Papers, 1832-1863*, ed. Donald Mackenzie Brown (Berkeley, 1947), p. 13.

[37] Dakin, *Scotch Paisano*, p. 52.

Long Beach by the Massachusetts-born John Temple, is the largest and most splendid extant adobe in southern California.[38] Excepting these several houses, architectural construction languished south of Santa Barbara until the early 1850's, when a number of cattlemen erected Monterey Colonial adobes from profits earned in supplying the demands of beef-hungry miners. And it was at one of these houses that Helen Hunt Jackson stayed while gathering materials for her famous novel of life in Old California.

Although relatively few Monterey Colonial houses were constructed in the years immediately preceding annexation, their widespread distribution is one explanation for the false conception of the two-story, veranda-sheltered adobe as the typical dwelling of the colonial period. And if most of the Spanish-Mexicans were too conservative, or too poor, to emulate American building standards, the Vallejo Adobe (Plate 5) and the Blue Wing Tavern in Sonoma testify to the accuracy with which provincials outside of Monterey could copy the hipped roof and veranda of the Larkin prototype. The Castro Adobe at San Juan Bautista (Plate 6) and the Casa de los Danas at the present village of Nipomo, San Luis Obispo County, illustrate the occasional use of Greek Revival refinements in the construction of inland Monterey Colonial houses. The latter, built by Captain William Goodwin Dana, uncle of the author of *Two Years before the Mast* and one of the earliest New England residents in California, was undoubtedly owner-designed, for Dana is listed in Bancroft's "Pioneer Register" as architect as well as trader, soapmaker, physician, and trapper.

José Amador, with the aid of Robert Livermore, constructed a two-story adobe on his 16,000-acre Rancho San Ramón in Contra Costa County in the late thirties. At the present site of Berkeley, José Domingo Peralta, a member of a famous building family of the Mexican period, began a long series of adobe alterations, which culminated during the American period in a frame house of timber traditionally said to have been shipped around Cape Horn from New England. Farther up the coast at the site of the Russian settlement of Kuskoff near Bodega

[38] Parks, "In Pursuit of Vanished Days," pp. 19-20.

Bay, Captain Stephen Smith, a native of Maryland, constructed a two-story, redwood-frame adobe that has been described as having a porch along the front and dormer windows opening at the upper story onto a balcony. And in Petaluma, the northernmost area of provincial settlement, the vast shingled roof and far-spreading verandas of the Vallejo Adobe testify to the nearly limitless reaches to which the Monterey Colonial style could be extended (Plate 5). This extant fortress-hotel, the largest adobe structure in California, was constructed without the use of nails and has mud walls built to a depth of four feet in order to carry the weight of redwood beams used in floor and roof framing.[39]

In the colonial period California was a sea frontier, and settlement was limited largely to the coastal area between San Diego and Fort Ross. In the absence of any need for civic or commercial construction, the colonial builders were concerned only with shelter. The wide disparity between the authentic dwelling of the Spanish-Mexican and the romantic legend of a splendid manorial architecture indicates the falsity of the larger myth of a Spanish Colonial civilization in California. And yet, lacking in aesthetic importance, primitive and poor though it is, the work of the adobe builders has the merit of faithfully interpreting the pastoral and isolated life of provincial California. The single important architectural innovation in this period was the fusion of the adobe and wood building traditions at Monterey. But this compromise was short-lived, and by the time of annexation the American frame house was the vernacular architecture of the Yankee-dominated settlements in California.

[39] J. N. Bowman, "The Peraltas and Their Houses," *CHSQ*, XXX (Sept. 1951), 217-231; Marion Randall Parsons, *Old California Houses* (Berkeley, 1952), pp. 14-15; Giffen, "Two-Story Adobe," p. 21.

II. THE PIONEER BUILDERS

T HOMAS LARKIN's architectural innovations proved as significant for California social history as his merchandising methods. Together they demonstrate that American cultural and economic supremacy preceded military conquest and political annexation. For if the climate and availability of materials on the California frontier permitted each successive wave of immigrants to practice an instinctive colonialism, only the Americans brought with them a culture capable of winning and holding the land. The Monterey Colonial house symbolizes the brief period of compromise between the competing Spanish-Mexican and the American colonial cultures; the Yankee frame house represents the decade of social and political change beginning in 1841 and ending in the gold rush during which California became American. The winning of the architectural frontier by American pioneer builders constituted one of the first victories in the conquest of California.

In every sense the Spanish-Mexicans proved incapable of maintaining their initial advantage on the Pacific frontier. At the time of annexation in 1846 California had a population of hardly eight settlers for every mile of coast line; some eight million acres of its land wealth were in the possession of a mere eight hundred grantees. In the absence of Mexican emigrants to colonize the land, or Mexican capital to develop its resources and trade, the fate of the province rested in the inexperienced hands of the *Californianos*, who, as Richard Henry Dana reported from personal experience, "are an idle, thriftless people, and can make nothing for themselves."[1]

An examination of the actual state of adobe building demonstrates the truth of this observation for architecture; the contemporary reports of foreign travelers and the journals of prominent merchants testify to its economic validity. For despite their lordly landholdings, the Spanish-Mexicans were themselves victims of the same "lotos-land lethargy" that limited the culture of the coastal Indians to bare survival. Not only did the provincials exchange immense tracts of land for the services of Yankee carpenters and mechanics, but they used their own agricultural acreage so carelessly that the colony was sometimes on the edge of starvation. Although living in a country rich in vineyards and famous for its cattle, the *rancheros* ordered wine from Boston and purchased, at greatly inflated prices, shoes made from their own cowhides shipped twice around the Horn. Even the celebrated "Spanish" shawls of Old California were pieces of Chinese silk carried to the colony in New England vessels.

By 1846 Americans constituted the chief foreign element in California; they controlled the economic life of the colony and composed its strongest military force. Their leaders, mainly New England merchants and landowners, effected by marriage and interest the closest ties with the ruling provincial families. How crucial this was in keeping the peace in the critical first half of the pioneer decade is evident in the success attained by Abel Stearns, son-in-law to Don Juan Bandini, in quieting the fears of Governor Micheltorena when Commodore Thomas ap Catesby Jones seized Monterey in 1842 under the impression that the United States was at war with Mexico. Four years later Jacob Leese proved as adroit in soothing the pride of his father-in-law, General Mariano Guadalupe Vallejo, when the Mexican commander was seized in the abortive Bear Flag rebellion. Given this mutuality of interest and the utter poverty of Mexican arms and ideas, it is not surprising that actual annexation was accomplished with relatively the same ease that distinguished the earlier transition from Spanish empire to Mexican republic.

[1] *Two Years before the Mast*, p. 94.

In a revealing speech before the local assembly on the eve of annexation, Governor Pío Pico candidly summed up the results of a half century of American economic and cultural penetration:

> We find ourselves threatened by hordes of Yankee emigrants . . . whose progress we cannot arrest. Already have the wagons of that perfidious people scaled the almost inaccessible summits of the Sierra Nevada, crossed the entire continent, and penetrated the fruitful valley of the Sacramento. . . . Already . . . [they] are cultivating farms, establishing vineyards, erecting mills, sawing up lumber, and doing a thousand other things which seem natural to them.[2]

The overland pioneers singled out by Governor Pico for special abuse represented a minority of the foreign residents in California at the time of annexation. For though the reports of the extraordinary wanderings of Jedediah Strong Smith and James Pattie increased the number of emigrant wagons crossing the Sierra passes between 1840 and 1846, the majority of the survivors of the Overland Route settled in the Oregon Territory. Despite the dramatic interlude of the western mountain men, California remained a sea frontier, and its life and architecture in the first half of the nineteenth century reflected a maritime immigration.

Brief though it was, the era of the mountain men did not pass wholly unmirrored in pioneer building. In something of the same manner in which the palisade house was the earliest permanent Spanish shelter, the traditional log cabin served in the interior of California as a first makeshift dwelling. Some notable examples were the rude shelter erected by General John Bidwell along the Sacramento River at the present site of Marysville and the Kentucky blockhouse constructed by George Yount in Sonoma in 1836. Another log stockade—fashioned in the form of a parallelogram with walls made of cottonwood, willow trunks, and log houses fitted with "loopholes, bastions at the corners, and indentured gateways"—was erected in 1851 at the site of San Bernardino by Mormon settlers for protection from Indian attack. The Tennessee backwoodsman Isaac Graham constructed a log cabin near San

---

[2] As quoted in Titus Fey Cronise, *The Natural Wealth of California* (San Francisco, 1868), p. 51.

Juan Bautista in which he was living when the young Californian Juan Bautista Alvarado enlisted his support in the successful revolution of 1836; how many of his band of *rifleros Americanos* dwelt in similar shelters is not known. Certainly there were a number of wilderness cabins such as those built in the forties by Elias Barnett in the Napa Valley and Turner Elder at Dry Creek in San Joaquin County.[3]

One explanation for the dearth of log cabins in California is that this kind of structure required so great a supply of timber that its construction was necessarily limited to the heavily forested areas of the coast range, the Sierra foothills, and the high valleys. Not only are there important exceptions to this generalization—notably the colonization of New Hope on the Stanislaus River in the sparsely wooded San Joaquin Valley in 1846, where a party of New York Mormons erected a log house "constructed after the Western manner and covered with oak shingles" and floored with roughhewn boards—but subsequent building in the richly forested mining regions to the east and to the north of the great central valley produced relatively few log cabins.[4] And the improvised board shelters erected during the gold rush were replaced by the traditional American frame house as soon as the miners turned to the problem of permanent dwellings. Some early examples of the transition from log to clapboard housing in the mid-forties are the dozen wilderness cabins reported in the Napa Valley, all of which were replaced within a year by their builders.[5]

That the New England frame house, and not the log cabin, was the typical American dwelling on the California frontier at the time of the gold rush testifies to the common Yankee background of the colonial and pioneer builders. Although Bancroft's "Pioneer Register" is incomplete in recording places of origin, it nonetheless suggests the preponderance of New Englanders and "upstate" New Yorkers among the foreign

[3] Parsons, p. 69; "The Chronicles of George C. Yount," p. 54; Hero Eugene and Ethel Grace Rensch, *Historic Spots in California: The Southern Counties* (Stanford, 1932), pp. 151-152; Dakin, *Hartnell*, pp. 210-211; H. E. and E. G. Rensch and Mildred (Brooke) Hoover, *Historic Spots in California: Valley and Sierra Counties* (Stanford, 1933), p. 351.

[4] Rensch and Hoover, *Valley and Sierra Counties*, pp. 358-359.

[5] Hoover, *Counties of the Coast Range*, p. 288.

residents in provincial California. The record left by W. F. Swasey, a Maine man and overlander of 1845, is a better source for a study of the self-renewing nature of Yankee immigration in the first half of the last century. Among sixty-three Americans important in territorial affairs prior to 1849, fifty-eight are listed as natives of New England or New York in Swasey's *The Early Days and Men of California*. As the following chapter demonstrates, 85 per cent of the American architects in the gold rush came from New England, New York, and Pennsylvania. In the case of the California builders at least, it is difficult to dispute Henry L. Dawes's statement that larger portions of the United States have been settled by New Englanders than by any other regional group, and wherever New Englanders have gone "they have carried with them the life and characteristics of New England."[6]

Elam Brown, who milled the first lumber in the San Antonio redwood groves, and William B. Ide, who interrupted his trade as a carpenter to share leadership with John Charles Frémont in the Bear Flag movement, are typical of the pioneer builders who left old homes in New England and New York to create an American dependency on the Pacific. But aggressive as these pioneers were as individual colonizers and builders, it is doubtful that the Yankee frame house could have become the California vernacular architecture within a year of annexation were it not for the major Mormon and military migrations of the forties. The thirty "artisans" employed by Captain John A. Sutter in his shops and mills at Sacramento, as well as the building fraternity of twenty-six carpenters, six brickmakers, and several painters who transformed the settlement of Yerba Buena into the Yankee village of San Francisco, were probably recruited from the several hundred Mormons who arrived in 1846 under the leadership of Samuel Brannan, from the Mormon Battalion, and from the youthful volunteers of Colonel Stevenson's New York battalion, all chosen for their "good character and skill in the industrial arts."[7]

[6] As quoted in Howard Allen Bridgman, *New England in the Life of the World* (Boston, 1920), p. 20.

[7] Coman, *Economic Beginnings*, II, 204, 216, 235; John Shertzer Hittell, *A History of the City of San Francisco* (San Francisco, 1878), p. 112; Bancroft, *History of California*, V, 499-500.

The pioneer builders constructed their dwellings in the historic heavy-frame technique, joining together by mortises and tenons a shell of massive timbers. An example of such construction is the two-story house built by Samuel Brannan of redwood milled at Corte Madera in 1847 and illustrated in Plate 8. Brannan's house, fitted with green shutters and a veranda, was the most substantial of the approximately one hundred frame buildings reported in San Francisco on the eve of the discovery of gold.[8] Though nothing remains of the "American model" farmhouses of "most comfortable and neat appearance" found in the region from the Sacramento Valley south to Santa Barbara, documented examples of heavy-frame construction exist in areas other than San Francisco. These include the large dwelling built by Albert Toomes in Monterey in 1845, three houses of redwood put up the same year in San Jose, and the two-story, twelve-room house constructed by the carpenter William Bushton in Monterey in 1847 of timber cut and notched in Australia.[9]

The most important building erected in the pioneer period was Colton Hall (Plate 7), begun in Old Monterey in 1847 by the American minister and mayor, Walter Colton. Although badly mutilated by reconstruction in 1915, this extant structure, with a two-story portico of unfluted, Ionic-type columns supporting a simple wood pediment, reflects the supremacy of Greek Revival architecture in the United States at mid-century. Constructed of materials of local origin and plastered over in imitation cut stone, Colton Hall was built by a labor levy made in the town's gambling and drinking dens. Among the reluctant workers Colton was fortunate in securing the services of a highly skilled English stonecutter, who is responsible for the excellent fittings of the foundation and walls. Describing this "bit of New England" on the Pacific Coast, the builder remarked that though it would attract little consideration in the eastern states, "in California it is without a rival."[10]

[8] J. S. Hittell, *History of San Francisco*, pp. 87, 117.

[9] Bryant, pp. 246, 423; San Jose *News*, Jan. 26, 1917; "Adobes and Old Buildings," pp. 64-67.

[10] George Tays, "Colton Hall" (1936), passim, MS in the Bancroft Library; Newcomb, *Old Mission Churches*, pp. 339, 342; Walter Colton, *Three Years in California* (New York, 1850), p. 356.

With the completion of Colton Hall, the labors of New Englanders at Monterey to conquer California's commerce and to create a secular architecture had ended. The rediscovery of the bay of San Francisco, into which drain the river systems of the western slopes of the Sierra Nevada, focused national and regional attention upon Yerba Buena, which at the time of Larkin's architectural compromise was distinguished only as the site of an Indian *temascal* and as a hunting ground for panther and grizzly bear. Here in July 1836 the American Jacob Leese erected the first structure in what was destined to be the foremost city of California. Leese's house, constructed of redwood brought by boat from Monterey and described somewhat grandly as a "mansion," measured sixty by twenty-five feet and appears to have been constructed of clapboards and roofed with shingles. Since the building was put up in three days, it was perhaps the first prefabricated house in California and the precursor of a bizarre succession of imported dwellings from the eastern seaboard, England, Hawaii, Australia, and China.[11]

Yerba Buena, known as San Francisco from 1847 on, was described at the beginning of the pioneer period by Nicholas "Cheyenne" Dawson as a seafaring village "mostly built of wood" whose houses were American in their architecture.[12] In addition to Leese's house, these dwellings included "a shanty of rough boards put up by a man named Richardson," Juan Fuller's washhouse, and Vioget's tavern, where the Yankees came to drink brandy and rant against Whigs.[13] The small frame house that sheltered the family of Benjamin Kelsey was the first pioneer household in California. In both dwelling and background the Kelseys present an all too rarely recorded contrast between the harsh conditions of the traditional American wilderness and the comfortable life of the New England merchant settled on the California frontier. While Thomas Larkin traded otter skins for Boston manufactures and

[11] Bancroft, *California Pastoral*, in *Works*, XXXIV (San Francisco, 1888), 726; J. S. Hittell, *History of San Francisco*, pp. 82-85; Frank Soulé, *The Annals of San Francisco* (New York, 1855), p. 168.

[12] As quoted in William Martin Camp, *San Francisco: Port of Gold* (Garden City, N.Y., 1947), p. 47.

[13] Richard Henry Dana, as quoted in Felix Riesenberg, *Golden Gate* (New York, 1940), p. 46.

quietly paved the way for peaceful annexation, Benjamin Kelsey hunted grizzly around the bay of San Francisco, and his wife Nancy, the friend of Frémont and Kit Carson, sewed the Bear Flag of the revolutionary California Republic. Whereas William Goodwin Dana presented his distinguished father-in-law, Don Carlos Antonio Carrillo, with twenty-one grandchildren, the Kelsey's daughter, carried as a baby across the Sierra passes in October 1841, died of head wounds as a result of an Indian scalping party.

Within a year of annexation San Francisco was the chief port of California, and "snug frame buildings" stood "glittering in whitewash and fresh paint" where ten years before Leese's redwood house stood alone among the dunes.[14] The San Franciscans, of whom there were perhaps nine hundred by the end of 1847, celebrated the new year of 1848 with a barrage of propaganda regarding "The Prospects of California" and settled down to grow rich as the country gradually filled up. But 1848 was California's year of destiny. Gold, discovered in January by James W. Marshall, a worker employed in Captain Sutter's sawmill at Coloma, suddenly and forever destroyed pastoral California with its several brisk little ports and its dependence upon the hide and tallow trade; the old order, changing under half a century of contact with Yankee sealers, merchants, and farmers, became extinct overnight in large areas of the territory. The effect upon architecture was accurately foretold by Emerson in a journal entry for January 1849:

> Suddenly the Californian soil is spangled with a little gold-dust . . . the news flies here and there, to New York, to Maine, to London, and an army of a hundred thousand picked volunteers, the ablest and keenest and boldest that could be collected, instantly organize and embark for this desart [sic], bringing tools, instruments, books, and framed houses, with them.[15]

California architecture in the period between the discovery of gold in 1848 and the end of the pioneer decade in 1851 presents a faithful picture of the transient, reckless, and improvising spirit of the times. In-

[14] Bancroft, *California Pastoral*, p. 741.
[15] Ralph Waldo Emerson, *Journals*, VIII (Boston, 1912), 7.

deed, in no other area are the pressures of immigration, inflation, and the waste from fire, flood, and failure incident to mining so manifest. In the scramble for gold, building was reduced to a question of shelter. For even if the architects who came in '49 and '50 represented substantially the same Yankee stock and traditions as did their predecessors, the gold-rush builders were able to shed cultural conservatism as rapidly as family ties and legal conventions. And though the California architectural renaissance was only several years away, the forty-niners housed them-selves in caves, brush arbors, blanket lean-tos, salvaged tents, wooden cabins, and, at best, imported iron and frame houses.

Building costs in the period of the gold rush were as uncertain and inflationary as the price of an egg or a laundered shirt. Lumber sold in 1849-1850 for as high as one dollar a square foot and bricks at one dollar apiece. At that time a simple one-story house of clapboard and shingles cost approximately $15,000 to build in San Francisco; a two-story hotel in San Jose cost $100,000. And despite excessive costs, available building materials were often poor in quality and unsuited to the purpose for which they were contracted.

In 1849 the average wage for labor in the mines was $16.00 a day; in 1850 it was $10.00. In the absence of any demand for the services of professional architects, most of the pioneer designers worked as carpenters at $16.00-$20.00 a day; similar talents brought only $12.00 in San Francisco. The inequality between coastal and inland wages in the building trades precipitated the first labor dispute in California: a strike of San Francisco carpenters and joiners in the winter of 1849 for wages equivalent to those prevailing at the mines. The temporary and unprofessional nature of the gold-rush labor force is demonstrated in the vocational backgrounds of this group of thirty striking "carpenters," which included three ministers, two lawyers, three physicians, and six bookkeepers.

The exorbitant building costs of the early gold era were naturally reflected in high rents and a minimum of space and privacy. In the winter of 1849 a two-story house in the Sierra rented for $500 a month and a room for $100; sleeping space in a San Francisco canvas or frame hotel, usually shared with a multitude of fleas and rats, was even higher than at the mines. The second story of the Parker House was leased to gamblers in 1849 for $60,000 a year, and a mercantile firm paid $40,000 annually to rent a one-story shop with a twenty-foot frontage on Montgomery Street. The Reverend James Woods, who preached his first sermon in Stockton in January 1850 in a tattered tent, considered himself extremely fortunate in obtaining, for only $100 a month, a "very slight frame, with shingle roof, and undressed plank floor."[16]

Whatever success the pioneer builder might have in overcoming the uncertainties of a day-to-day labor force, violently fluctuating building costs, and material inadequacies, he was still left with the most hazardous of investments, for the frame and canvas architecture of the gold rush proved to be "as inflammable as the temper of the inhabitants." Between 1849 and 1851 fire repeatedly swept through the pioneer communities, resulting in a total state property loss of more than $65,000,000. San Francisco framed the state's first building ordinance after the heart of the tent city was destroyed in May 1850. This measure, which prohibited the construction of cotton cloth structures, was the basis for an ordinance adopted by the San Jose town council in the same year forbidding the erection of canvas, willow, or cotton cloth buildings in the business district.

Either the miner could not, or would not, provide himself with proper housing. A description of Jacksonville, Amador County, in 1850 is given at length not only because it furnishes an architectural inventory of gold-rush housing, but also because it serves to catalogue the total inadequacy of pioneer standards of shelter, sanitation, and comfort:

> As in every other settlement, the houses are of every possible variety. . . . Most of these, even in winter, are tents. Some throw up logs a few feet high, filling up with clay between the logs. The tent is then stretched above, forming a roof. . . . Those who have more regard to their own comfort or health, erect log or stone houses, covering them with thatch or shingles. . . . Some comfortable wigwams are made of pine boughs thrown up in a conical form, and are quite dry. Many

---

[16] James Woods, *Recollections of Pioneer Work in California* (San Francisco, 1878), p. 22.

only spread a piece of canvas, or a blanket, over some stakes above them, while not a few make holes in the ground, where they burrow like foxes. . . . The Mexicans and Chilinos [sic] put up rude frames, which they cover with hides.[17]

This is obviously not architecture; it is hardly even housing. But when it is considered that 75 per cent of the state's population in 1850 was registered as engaged in mining, presumably living under conditions such as described above, a consideration of the state of shelter in the Sierra communities is essential to a faithful record of California life in the late pioneer period.

The desolation of the mining camps would be difficult to picture were it not for observations recorded during the gold rush. Restored Columbia, with its tree-lined streets and brick buildings, represents the town as it was rebuilt after the fire of 1854 and obviously suggests nothing of that camp of 1851 whose dwellings were constructed of "shakes, mud and stone, clapboard and adobe . . . having the ground for a floor and a dried bullock's hide in place of a door."[18] Nor can there be found in any of the other well-publicized Sierra hamlets of today the slightest evidence of the improvised tents and plank hovels, "formed of pine boughs, and covered with old calico shirts," of which Dame Shirley wrote in her letters of the same year.[19] An authentic picture of the shelters of the mountain camps can be pieced together only by turning from the later romanticists to the stark and often bitter pioneer records.

Generalizing about gold-era mountain hamlets, Bancroft has written that "the picturesque faded fast as the foliage fringe round the white-peaked tents was reduced to shorn stumps, midst unsightly mounds of earth, despoiled river-beds, and denuded slopes."[20] In 1849 Mrs. Royce described the buildings of one mining camp as "tents and cloth houses . . . occasionally a shanty, half logs and half boards, and one or

[17] Daniel B. Woods, *Sixteen Months at the Gold Diggings* (New York, 1851), p. 121.
[18] Edna Bryan Buckbee, *The Saga of Old Tuolumne* (New York, 1935), p. 95.
[19] Louise Amelia Knapp (Smith) Clappe, *The Shirley Letters from the California Mines, 1851-1852*, ed. Carl I. Wheat (New York, 1949), pp. 30-31.
[20] *History of California*, VI, 434.

two very inferior board houses."[21] A pioneer El Dorado physician found Sonora, the leading gold town in 1850, a jumble of flimsy shacks without a single chimney or proper fireplace; contemporary records of Auburn and Nevada City picture the buildings of these communities as a mixture of frame houses, dingy canvas shacks, and log cabins. Borthwick's somewhat later sketch of the buildings of Mokelumne Hill as largely "skeletons clothed in dirty rags of canvass" is typical enough to be final.[22]

The dismal state of gold-rush architecture resulted in part from the seasonal nature of placer mining and the confidence of the miners that they would win fortunes before winter dampened their hastily improvised shelters. Whether or not disappointment in this respect was general, large numbers of adventurers did retreat to lower elevations with the first winter storms and the flooding of the mines and sluices. It can be assumed, however, that at least a number of those who remained to fret out a mountain winter in sickness, loneliness, and discomfort replaced their temporary caves, arbors, and tents with some kind of timbered shacks.

The term log cabin is used frequently by pioneer chroniclers to describe the Sierra shelters of the gold era. And, as Plate 10 demonstrates, genuine log houses with notched ends and mud-chinked walls were erected occasionally among the frame and cloth dwellings that made up the typical mining communities of the early fifties. The first "cabin" in Tuolumne County is said to have been constructed of stripped young pine; Alonzo Delano and Lucius Fairchild recorded construction of proper log cabins on the Feather River in 1849. Sometimes the "log cabins" proved to be nothing more than timbered lean-tos, such as the huts thrown up the same year near Jackson with walls and roofs of rough slabs with the bark left on the outer side. Generally, however, the miners constructed their dwellings in the frame manner and covered them with rough boarding and hand-split shingles. The George Perkins Cabin (Plate 9), reconstructed for the California Midwinter Fair in San

[21] Sarah (Bayliss) Royce, *A Frontier Lady* (New Haven, 1932), p. 128.
[22] J. D. Borthwick, *Three Years in California* (London, 1857), p. 288.

Francisco in 1894, is typical of the gold-rush "log house" whose floor was generally the earth of the site and whose furnishings were a built-in bunk, a packing-case table, and a log bench.[23]

Though the American miners learned from the Mexicans how to construct brush huts, or *ramadas,* and though the towns of Auburn and Hornitos were laid out around a Spanish-style plaza, colonial building traditions were less prevalent at the mines than in any other section of the state. Sonora, an important exception, was founded by silver miners from the Mexican state of that name. Its buff and blue painted adobe buildings, hung with balconies and outside staircases, testified to the origin of its builders. By 1850, however, Sonora was no longer a Mexican camp. The legally minded Anglo-Saxons had driven the unfortunate Mexicans, together with the Chinese and other unpopular "foreigners," from the diggings by a combination of personal violence and a foreign miner's tax. Aliens to the adobe tradition, the triumphant lawgivers fashioned their makeshift shelters from Indian huts or along the lines of the shake and plank cabins of the California pioneers of the early forties.

Urban construction in gold-rush California did not differ significantly from that in the mining communities. San Francisco, "a bawdy, bustling bedlam of mudholes and shanties," is pictured in contemporary sources as an ugly crescent of Mexican adobes, frame structures imported in sections from New England, a smaller number of iron houses shipped from Europe and Asia, and a mass of canvas tents and shanties; Sacramento was a sprawling village of twoscore frame buildings, three hundred cloth houses, and several campfires under the trees.[24] Here in 1849, A. C. Sweetser undertook some of the earliest professional building in the territory by using willow poles for structural parts and canvas and tarred paper for roofing and wall coverings. It is probable that Sweetser constructed the long-remembered "Round Tent," whose attractions were listed by one scandalized forty-niner as an enormous bar and a col-

---

[23] Buckbee, p. 19; Lucius Fairchild, *California Letters,* ed. Joseph Schafer (Madison, 1931), p. 46; Rensch and Hoover, *Valley and Sierra Counties,* p. 22; John Walton Caughey, *Gold Is the Cornerstone* (Berkeley, 1948), p. 181; Bancroft, *History of California,* VI, 389.

[24] Herbert Asbury, *The Barbary Coast* (Long Beach, 1949), p. 18.

lection of obscene pictures in an atmosphere whose "naked, unmasked depravity" could be pictured only by the pen of a Cruikshank.[25]

The rapidity with which the gold-rush communities changed their architectural character makes any generalization regarding pioneer urban building, even from month to month, exceedingly hazardous. In December 1849 a traveler noted, "Of all the marvelous phases of the history of the Present, the growth of San Francisco is the one which will most tax the belief of the Future."[26] In that city in the summer of 1849 the only important buildings were an adobe city hall and customhouse, a brick structure on the corner of Washington and Powell streets, a public hospital accommodating three hundred patients, the two-story Parker House, and the El Dorado, the celebrated gambling den located in a tent on Portsmouth Square. By autumn of the same year a visitor reported that building was proceeding at the rate of one hundred structures a month, including "imposing edifices" of frame or brick construction, such as the building erected by William Heath Davis of materials brought from Boston and leased to the government for $36,000 a year.[27]

The flamboyant nature of public life in the mining communities has been the subject of many pioneer journals and reminiscences. And it is undeniable that in architecture, too, the glories of the gold-rush cities were the gambling and drinking halls and not the occasional brick warehouse or frame church. The change that the gold rush effected in the character of these places of masculine pleasure was recorded by a literate miner in a diary entry from San Francisco in October 1849, in which the fog-soaked canvas halls of an earlier summer visit are contrasted with the "magnificent saloons," replete with wine, entertainment, music "by the most accomplished and able professors of the art," and paintings "such as my pen may not describe."[28] Fortunately, a scene such as this

[25] An Illustrated History of Sacramento County, California (Chicago, 1890), p. 567; John Frederick Morse, The First History of Sacramento City, Written in 1853 (Sacramento, 1945), pp. 31-32.

[26] Bayard Taylor, Eldorado (New York, 1850), II, 55.

[27] J. S. Hittell, History of San Francisco, pp. 146-147; William Heath Davis, Sixty Years in California (San Francisco, 1889), p. 521.

[28] Woods, Sixteen Months, p. 168.

was captured by the pen of the British artist Frank Marryat, and the result is a delightful sketch of a metropolitan gambling hall in which pleasure-bent and bearded miners, sombreroed Mexicans, and quaintly garbed Chinese gamble and drink in outlandish contrast to gilt-worked ceilings, glass and mirrored columns, and enormous French paintings of nude women.[29]

In combating mud, rats, material shortages, and building costs, the Californians exhibited a talent for architectural improvisation that was typical of the exuberant spirit of the gold rush. In the winter of 1849-1850, when fifty inches of rain are said to have fallen on San Francisco and floods reduced Sacramento to an isolated "Venetian Lagoon," a sidewalk of flour sacks, cooking stoves, tobacco boxes, and pianos was laid out in San Francisco on the west side of Montgomery Street between Clay and Jackson. It was necessary to pick a path with extreme care over this walk because some of the stove covers were missing. Such makeshift construction was duplicated occasionally in the foundations of gold-rush buildings. In 1849 a house was erected on the mud flats at Jackson Street with foundations of large boxes of Virginia tobacco instead of the usual wooden piles. Before the building was completed, however, a fluctuation in the market price of tobacco made the foundations more valuable than the entire structure.[30]

At San Francisco in 1847 Emmanuel Russ erected one of the first California hotels out of planks salvaged from ships' bunks. Two years later the city hall of Stockton was lodged in an "unpretending brig" with the poop deck serving as courtroom, the hold converted into a prison, and the forecastle fitted up as a hospital. By 1849 enterprising builders had turned to the hundreds of deserted ships lying in the bay of San Francisco for living space and building materials. In August of that year the city of San Francisco purchased the brig *Euphemia* and converted it into a jail; the storeship *Apollo* was floated to a pier and reconstructed as a saloon and lodginghouse. Among other vessels eventually

---

[29] *Mountains and Molehills* (New York, 1855), p. 43.

[30] James R. Garnis, "Early Days of San Francisco" (1887), p. 14, MS in the Bancroft Library; Theodore Augustus Barry and B. A. Patten, *Men and Memories of San Francisco, in the "Spring of '50"* (San Francisco, 1873), p. 91.

embedded in the mud flats as living quarters was the ship *Niantic*, which anchored in the spring of '49 at the present corner of Clay and Sansome streets with two hundred fifty Panamanian immigrants. This subsequently became the Ship Hotel, which, at the time it was sketched by Frank Marryat in 1850, had been converted into a two-story clapboard structure roofed with shingles (Plate 11).[31]

Among the notable architectural novelties resorted to in the desperate search for living space were prefabricated sheet-metal buildings imported from all parts of Europe and Asia. Iron houses and warehouses, manufactured by E. T. Bellhouse of Manchester and John Walker of London, were imported to California in numbers in 1849. The forty corrugated-iron buildings of English origin then reported in San Francisco, a dozen of which are said to have been the property of the early millionaire James Lick, were presumably from these manufacturers. In the autumn of 1849 Taylor claimed that at least seventy-five prefabricated iron houses had been imported from Canton and erected in California by Chinese carpenters. The forty-niner James Barnes recalled putting up several one-room iron houses in Sacramento in November 1850, and another in the immediate neighborhood in the following year; in Los Angeles the one recorded iron house was of English origin and stood at the corner of Court and Spring streets. Milton Little set up four iron houses in Monterey in 1851 using galvanized iron imported from New York and wooden frames shipped from Australia; the same year an iron-covered church of Gothic design and plastered in imitation stone was erected in San Francisco on the north side of Pine Street.[32]

There was apparently considerable architectural variety in the design of these iron houses. An example of the corrugated, story-and-a-half type is illustrated in Plate 18 to the left of the Montgomery Block. This

[31] [Leonard Kip], *California Sketches* (Albany, N.Y., 1850), p. 18; Soulé, p. 233; Marryat, sketch facing p. 48.

[32] Henry Russell Hitchcock, *Early Victorian Architecture in Britain* (New Haven, 1954), I, 527; San Francisco *Examiner*, Feb. 12, 1893, p. 17; Taylor, *Eldorado*, I, 111; "Life, Adventures and Experiences in California, Being the Letters of James Barnes, 1849-57," pp. 38, 47-48, MS in the Bancroft Library; Guinn, "Los Angeles in the Adobe Age," *HSSCQ*, IV (1897), 49; "Adobes and Old Buildings," p. 98; *Alta California*, Jan. 23, 1852.

particular structure, photographed in 1856, is possibly one of the buildings imported from England by James Lick. One observer insists that the California iron houses were painted brown; another that they were painted white after the example of the traditional American frame house.[33] Sometimes the prefabricated metal buildings boasted such architectural refinements as diamond-shaped windowpanes, cast-iron canopies, and Gothic ornaments riveted over entrance doors and under roof eaves.

The number of prefabricated frame structures alleged to have been erected in the urban and mountain communities during the gold era is the subject of the most exaggerated speculation. It seems certain that the largest single order was the shipment of twenty-five houses that arrived in San Francisco from Boston in November 1849 aboard the *Oxnard*. These frames were consigned to the merchant William Howard, who presented one of them to the city as a shelter for California's first orphanage. In the summer of 1850 William Heath Davis purchased eight or ten prefabricated buildings from the cargo of the *Cybell*, out of Portland, Maine; somewhat later, Commodore Robert Field Stockton imported ten wooden houses and erected them in his Alameda Gardens subdivision near San Jose. A historian of San Francisco in the fifties records the existence of more than fifty such frame houses, "mustered in sections and fitted in Boston."[34]

Many of the frame houses imported into California during the gold rush were consigned for ultimate shipment to inland communities and isolated mountain hamlets. The first recorded dwellings in Stockton and Marysville were clapboard houses that arrived from the metropolis by river steamer after a sea journey around South America; one of the earliest frame structures in Sacramento was a substantial "Gothic cottage" trimmed with scrollwork and set up on L Street by a pioneer physician. Perhaps the most ambitious of the houses shipped to the mines was the Yankee-fitted mansion assembled by Samuel Brannan in 1849 on the

[33] Borthwick, p. 44; San Francisco *Chronicle*, June 19, 1887, p. 13.

[34] Barry and Patten, pp. 205-206; Davis, *Sixty Years*, pp. 533-534; Hoover, *Counties of the Coast Range*, p. 490; as quoted in Pauline Jacobson, *City of the Golden 'Fifties* (Berkeley, 1941), p. 69.

banks of the Feather River near Nicolaus and credited by local tradition with eight rooms and a winding staircase.[35]

Some of the difficulties incident to setting up an imported wooden house in the interior are recounted in the memoirs of the Swiss immigrant Heinrich Lienhard, who accepted as part payment for a $10,000 debt a Sacramento frame house valued at $2,000. Before his twenty-four-by-twenty-five-foot house was habitable, however, Lienhard paid a freight bill of $1,300 to have the parts floated up the Feather River and moved to his lot, engaged a pair of Yankee carpenters for $600 to assemble the frame, and was forced to purchase additional materials worth $800. When finally completed, the two-room structure had cost its bewildered owner $4,700.[36]

Prefabricated frame houses of New England origin were also imported into the southern counties during the gold rush. One of the first wood buildings south of Monterey is said to have been a frame structure shipped from Boston to San Pedro and dragged to Los Angeles by oxcart. The "quaint Georgian door and window frames" and the "Boston workmanship" of such houses as the Casa Santa Cruz can be cited as evidence of the advance of Yankee architectural components against the entrenched adobe tradition of southern California. These examples were rare, however; for, when the frame building for the Sisters of Charity arrived in Los Angeles in 1856, none of the local carpenters was equal to the assembling problem, and the church authorities were forced to send east for a competent workman.[37]

Typically New England in style and construction, the imported frame buildings of gold-rush California were invariably painted white with green shutters. The clapboard houses Howard erected south of Market Street in San Francisco had peaked roofs trimmed under the eaves with Gothic drippings and porches adorned with turned wood

[35] Bancroft, *History of California*, VI, 463-465; Barber and Baker, *Sacramento Illustrated* (Sacramento, 1950), p. 34; Rensch and Hoover, *Valley and Sierra Counties*, p. 465.

[36] *A Pioneer at Sutter's Fort*, 1846-1850, trans. and ed. Marguerite Knowlton (Eyre) Wilbur (Los Angeles, 1941), pp. 227-229.

[37] Guinn, "Los Angeles in the Adobe Age," p. 49; Rensch, *Southern Counties*, pp. 48-49; Harris Newmark, *Sixty Years in Southern California*, 1853-1913 (New York, 1916), p. 203.

balustrades. One of the houses purchased by Davis and shipped to San Diego for his own residence was a fair specimen of the symmetrical, colonial frame house that remained the American archetype until after the Civil War. It is possible that Judge Burritt's San Francisco house, described by Barry and Patten in 1851 as "a sweet bit of our old home spirited across the continent," was another of Davis' imported Maine frames.[38]

Representative examples of Yankee prefabricated houses of the early gold period are illustrated in Plates 13 and 16. The one at Angels Camp is the prototype California house for the period 1846-1869, and, until recently, many such structures could be seen in the mountain hamlets and on farms in the Sacramento and San Joaquin valleys. The general style of the Angels Camp house is Greek Revival, which remained the domestic vernacular on California's architectural frontier until after the completion of the Pacific railroad. The building to the extreme left in Plate 16 is similar to an imported frame house described by Barry and Patten.[39]

One of the few surviving examples of a Boston-fitted frame from the northernmost part of the state is the Greek Revival house at Shasta erected in 1851 by Dr. Benjamin Shurtleff, a native of Massachusetts and a graduate of Harvard College (Plate 14). This house, with its two-story central portico surmounted by a pediment and flanked by low porches, is reminiscent of the "academy" style used by Walter Colton at Monterey in 1847. The still solid foundations of the Shurtleff House are of rock and hand-hewn timbers; its clapboarding, mahogany staircase, and door- and window frames are of New England origin and were floated from San Francisco to Sacramento and then hauled to Shasta by ox team.[40]

The Parker House, erected on the old Spanish plaza in 1849, was either constructed of sections shipped from the East Coast or pieced together from imported materials. If the latter is true, the hotel was prob-

[38] Andrew F. Rolle, "William Heath Davis and the Founding of American San Diego," *CHSQ*, XXXI (Mar. 1952), 33-48; Barry and Patten, p. 31.

[39] Page 231.

[40] Edna B. Eaton, "The Shurtleff House—Shasta," *Covered Wagon*, III (May-June-July 1944), 39.

ably designed by Levi Goodrich, who is credited with the first work wrought in San Francisco by a professional architect. At any rate, some of the impatient and grandiose building conceptions of the gold rush are illustrated in the construction of this famous old hostelry, whose owners, when they discovered that the glass ordered for the windows was improperly cut, refused to reduce the size of the apertures and instead, according to local tradition, dispatched a fast sailing vessel to the Hawaiian Islands for accurately measured glass.[41]

Several years after the building of the Parker House the early San Francisco millionaire Jeremiah Clark erected a large imported frame on the corner of Chestnut and Hyde streets, which stood almost a century as a reminder of gold-rush building (Plate 17). Despite a Gothic aspect proclaimed by battlements and rope detailing over the window frames, this house, later sold to Captain Humphrey (or Humphries), represents the same American Colonial tradition as the Larkin House. In this respect Humphrey's house, with its symmetrical façade, fanlight and glass door panels, cupola, and horizontal wood siding, was typical of many so-called Gothic Revival structures of early California, whose basic colonial origin was scarcely disguised by the superimposition of currently fashionable medieval ornament.[42]

The most celebrated of existing imported buildings of the late pioneer period, as well as an unusually fine specimen of the less common Gothic Revival style, is the house General Vallejo erected at Sonoma in 1850-1851. Described in the nineteenth century as one of the few historic mansions of the Pacific Coast, Lachryma Montis (Tear of the Mountain) is said to have cost nearly $60,000, and with its South American bricks, Chinese iron, and mantelpieces from Honolulu, it is a good example of the kind of international effort that house building in the gold rush represented.[43]

[41] Ralph Herbert Cross, The Early Inns of California, 1844-1869 (San Francisco, 1954), Ch. viii.

[42] Eleanor Preston Watkins, The Builders of San Francisco and Some of Their Early Homes (San Francisco, 1935), pp. 20-23.

[43] Charles Howard Shinn, "Pioneer Spanish Families in California," Century Illustrated Monthly Magazine, XLI (Jan. 1891), 386; Myrtle Mason McKittrick, Vallejo, Son of California (Portland, Ore., 1944), pp. 303-304.

The religious congregations in the pioneer period were housed in Yankee frame structures differing neither in style nor construction from the more numerous sea-borne secular buildings. The era of worship under canvas, when the Baptists of San Francisco met beneath a roof made from old ships' sails, and the Presbyterians crowded into a tent formerly used as the marquee of a Massachusetts military company, merged quickly into one of prefabricated frame buildings. In 1849 the Methodist-Episcopal congregation of San Francisco was sheltered in a small frame structure shipped from Oregon; one Roman Catholic body met in a timbered house on Vallejo Street; and the Baptists gathered in a primitive clapboard and shingled house on Washington Street. In the summer of 1850 the Methodists in Nevada City put up a frame church, and the same year the San Francisco Presbyterians replaced their tent with a "neat Gothic edifice" designed and built in New York by J. Coleman Hart.[44]

In the decade beginning with large-scale milling operations in the coastal redwood groves in 1841 and ending in the gold rush, California became American. One of the first victories in the struggle between the mutually antagonistic Spanish-Mexican and American cultures was the triumph of Yankee building standards over those of the adobe builders. The discovery of gold in 1848 greatly accelerated American acculturation. But of the many improvisations that the demands of population, inflation, and material shortages forced upon the meager building resources of gold-rush California, only the prefabricated frame structures represented an enduring architectural tradition. And though the imported New England houses were significant in extending American building standards to the most isolated areas of the state, they hardly constituted a revolution in regional housing, for the work of the pioneer builders at Monterey and San Francisco had made California an American architectural frontier at the time of annexation.

---

[44] Soulé, pp. 233, 690-693; Helen Throop Purdy, *San Francisco, As It Was, As It Is, and How to See It* (San Francisco, 1912), p. 108; Charles P. Kimball, *San Francisco City Directory, 1850* (San Francisco, 1870), p. 127; William Taylor, *California Life Illustrated* (London, 1867), p. 56; William Branson Lardner and M. J. Brock, *History of Placer and Nevada Counties, California* (Los Angeles, 1924), p. 330.

III. THE GREAT IMMIGRATION

THE AGE of gold is treated traditionally as a short, lusty, and episodic chapter in California history, beginning with James Marshall's discovery at Coloma in 1848 and ending with the decline of placer mining five years later. In terms of population growth, economic development, and cultural achievement, however, it is part of a larger period of physical isolation and material prosperity that ended only in 1869 with the completion of the Pacific railroad. In this period six hundred thousand people came to California in the great immigration. And if few of the many who came in search of gold and silver found riches in the mines, those who stayed to trade, farm, and build gave California a cosmopolitan people and an international architecture.

One third of those who came in the great immigration took part in the gold rush—the most significant event in the development of nineteenth-century California architecture. For though construction in 1849 and 1850 was limited to the fabrication of tent shelters, wooden shacks, and imported iron and frame houses, gold provided the motivation that brought to an undeveloped and isolated country an unusually well-trained and talented body of designers and builders. Their presence in California at mid-century explains the state's unique exception to the cultural desolation of the mining frontier and accounts for the first flowering of western architecture in the two decades between the gold rush and the railroad.

In 1850, 75 per cent of California's population was American born.[1] Though some scholars continue to characterize the forty-niners as "crude American backwoodsmen brutalized and emotionally impoverished by their conquest of the West" and to insist that the state's antiforeign tendencies stem from southern traditions of racial inequality, there was no important frontier or Deep South immigration to California at any time in the last century.[2] How closely the Americans in the gold rush followed the historic pattern of Yankee colonization is evident from the fact that 40 per cent of them were from New England, New York, and Pennsylvania, and another 16 per cent from the Ohio Valley—an area where Yankee social and architectural traditions were exceptionally strong. True, the Seventh Census recorded one out of every five Americans in California in 1850 as southern. Further investigation, however, reveals that this minority emigrated largely from Kentucky, Virginia, and Maryland. When the great immigration ended in 1869, 70 per cent of the American-born Californians were from the northeastern and north-central United States.

Approximately 75 per cent of the architects in the gold rush were American born. This figure, based upon the records of thirty-two designers who are known to have reached the California frontier in 1849 and 1850, complements exactly the over-all population pattern as reported in the Seventh Census.[3] But whereas less than one half of the Americans in the gold rush emigrated from the northeastern states, 85 per cent of the architects came from New England, New York, and Pennsylvania, with the seaboard states of Massachusetts and Maine alone accounting for one third of their numbers. Further, though American numerical superiority in the architectural profession declined from

[1] For statistics relative to the great immigration see the Seventh, Eighth, and Ninth Censuses of the United States; and Commonwealth Club of California, San Francisco, *The Population of California: A Report of a Research Study Made by Authorization of the Board of Governors* (San Francisco, 1946).

[2] Paul Radin, "The Italians of San Francisco: Their Adjustment and Acculturation" (1935), pp. 28-30, abstract in the University of California Library, Berkeley.

[3] Biographical sources for California architects are collected in an appendix and will not be footnoted in the text.

75 per cent in 1851 to hardly 50 per cent in 1869, three fourths of this native-born body were from New England and New York. Thus architecture more than any other field except education justified the hopes of that Harvard president who exhorted the Massachusetts gold seekers to go forth into the wilderness with the "Bible in one hand and your New England civilization in the other and make your mark upon the people and the country."[4]

The character of the great immigration was extraordinarily masculine, youthful, and adventurous. In the spring of 1853, when the *Alta California* spoke of the number of "delicate and refined" women in San Francisco, "the Calypso whose presence makes the desert bloom, and reconciles even the shipwrecked Telemachus to a home not his own," men outnumbered women five to one.[5] And the niece of Francis Parkman and the cousin of James K. Polk notwithstanding, the "sisterhood of the boulevards by night" claimed the allegiance of most of the women of '49. The proud boast of an enthusiastic citizen of Sonora, "We have more gamblers, more drunkards, more ugly, bad women . . . than any other place of similar dimensions within Uncle Sam's dominions," was echoed in many California towns, where "the vision of a faithful wife darning socks over an evening fire is unthinkable."[6] Nor was this merely a temporary imbalance. When the period closed in 1869, the California population was still 70 per cent male.

Considered as a statistical average, the architects in the great immigration were talented men in their early twenties who spent a season or two in the mines and then settled down to comfortable practices in San Francisco or Sacramento. As individuals, however, they possessed a spirit of adventure and a capacity for improvisation that make them representative frontiersmen. Take, for example, the history of Matthew Teed, whose lust for adventure, sharpened in the Calaveras mines, drove him across New Mexico, on to the slopes of Pike's Peak, and

[4] Edward Everett, as quoted in Caughey, p. 81.

[5] *Alta California*, Mar. 4, 1853.

[6] As quoted in Remi A. Nadeau, *The Ghost Towns of California* (Los Angeles, 195–?), p. 34; Arthur Tysilio Johnson, *California: An Englishman's Impressions of the Golden State* (London, 1913), p. 70.

finally into the Elk City gold rush before he returned to his Stockton building practice. And there is Albert Snyder, son of a Virginia governor, who started his career in San Francisco in 1850 after several years devoted to the study of architecture in the course of which he begged his way through Italy, supported himself in Paris by manufacturing flower bouquets, and argued his way out of a London jail into which he was thrown as a thief and a vagabond.

Writing of the San Franciscans at mid-century, Frank Marryat claimed that "in no other community so limited could one find so many well-informed and clever men—men of all nations, who have added the advantages of traveling to natural abilities and a liberal education."[7] It is precisely this combination of training and experience that separated the California architects from the general American profession, whose standards were hardly distinguishable from the more advanced stages of carpentry. For if the academic background of George Nagle at Germantown College and John Lo Romer at Princeton was exceptional, most of the architects in the great immigration were professionally trained. Albert A. Bennett, the Quaker minister's son who arrived in 1849 and did much of the early building in the gold towns and later, as state architect, completed the capitol at Sacramento, studied for three years in a New York office; the Massachusetts-born Henry W. Cleaveland, disciple of Andrew Jackson Downing and author himself of *Village and Farm Cottages* (New York, 1856), brought to his California practice of the fifties and the sixties the advantages of European travel and eastern experience. The New Yorker Gordon P. Cummings, who achieved an unrivaled reputation among native architects in the decades prior to the coming of the railroad, and Stephen H. Williams, whose Parrott's Granite Block was the first great international building project in the West, are thought to have had extensive training in England and the eastern United States.

Many of the architects in the great immigration brought to their western practices not only a good measure of professional training, but a background that included some major eastern commissions. A. A.

[7] Page 38.

Bennett designed Orion Academy in Montgomery, Alabama; the celebrated Reuben Clark of Maine, who planned the United States Marine Hospital in San Francisco in 1853, had the advantage of an earlier commission for the Mississippi state capitol to aid him in work on the Sacramento Statehouse in 18611869. Nathaniel Dudley Goodell, who had acquired an education in carpentry at Amherst, Massachusetts, built the city hall at Belchertown and an entire mill town before the lure of gold brought him to Sacramento in 1849. Abraham Powell and John W. Bones are reputed to have practiced successfully in their native Philadelphia before coming west in the gold rush. The New Englander Seth Babson, chief architect for Charles Crocker and Leland Stanford, arrived in San Francisco in 1850 with building experience acquired at Newburyport, Massachusetts; Levi Goodrich, whose work ranged from adobe structures at the height of the gold rush to the neoclassic Santa Clara County Courthouse, designed the houses of Edward Channing and Miss Catherine Sedgwick at Stockbridge, Massachusetts, before beginning his apprenticeship in the New York office of R. G. Hatfield.

Of course, not all of the American architects who came to California between 1849 and 1869 were so well equipped. Some were members of the profession only by that generous extension of carpentry into the realm of design that was commonplace prior to the founding of the American Institute of Architects. Typical of these early architectbuilders were the New Englanders Albion C. Sweetser, whose father trained him in the craft before he came overland in '49, and J. O. McKee, whose trade was learned from a ship's carpenter aboard a sailing vessel en route to the gold fields. Charles S. Peck, one of the first architects known to have practiced at the mines, and Peter J. Barber, the leading designer in Santa Barbara, were sons and brothers of master builders. James E. Wolfe, interesting to historians as the architect of the San Francisco residence of Hubert Howe Bancroft and founder of the *California Architect and Building News*, learned his craft through a Maryland apprenticeship before coming west at the end of the gold rush. C. K. Garrison, mayor of San Francisco in 1854, was a builder of houses at West Point, New York; and William T. Coleman, leader of the famous Committee of Vigilance, set himself up in Sacramento in 1849 as a contractor-builder, willing to undertake any commission from "a dry-goods box to a block of buildings."[8]

In 1850, 25 per cent of California's population emigrated from outside the United States; by 1860 this minority had risen significantly to include 40 per cent of the state's inhabitants. And though external immigration subsided somewhat after the completion of the railroad, the average of foreign births to total population for the last half of the nineteenth century was an impressive 30 per cent. Architects in the great immigration follow almost exactly the general population pattern, and approximately one of every three designers on the California architectural frontier was foreign born. At least one half of these were British, a quarter were German, and the remainder came equally from France, Belgium, Switzerland, Scandinavia, and Mexico.

The Irish and the Chinese, although the largest foreign elements in the great immigration, contributed little to California architecture. Of fifteen designers known to have emigrated from the British Empire in the score of years between 1849 and 1869, only one was Irish. This was Thomas England, who collaborated with William Crain on old St. Mary's in San Francisco in 1853. The Reverend Father Quigley, in a curious and ill-informed contemporary study called *The Irish Race in California* (San Francisco, 1878), lists three hypothetical architects. One of these, Patrick J. O'Connor, "of the ancient stock of the O'Connors of Ballinagare," was nonetheless born in Liverpool; Thomas J. Welsh has proved to be a native of Australia; and the third, a William Corcoran, has left no record whatsoever.

Though legend insists that a "great" Chinese architect was brought over to supervise the construction of Parrott's Granite Block in San Francisco in 1852, and records exist of a "Chinese pavilion" at Placerville and "one perfect little temple beside the river at Marysville," nothing survives from this period to indicate any important activity by oriental

---

[8] Bancroft, *History of California*, VI, 766; James Augustin Brown Scherer, "*The Lion of the Vigilantes*": *William T. Coleman and the Life of Old San Francisco* (Indianapolis, 1939), p. 55.

designers.[9] How thoroughly the Chinese accepted American methods of construction is demonstrated in photographs of the old fishing village at Monterey, whose typically shantytown buildings belie the fact that the inhabitants "burn tapers before their gods on the rocks, and fish . . . in just such junks and small boats as may be seen at Hong-Kong and Canton."[10] The joss house at Fiddletown and the Chinese store at Angels Camp were conventional brick and stone buildings; the joss house at Dutch Flat was an adobe structure in the Mexican tradition; the Chinese Christian churches in Sacramento were typically American frame structures.[11] San Francisco's modern Chinatown, with its pagodas and scrollwork, brilliant red and gold paint, and authentic oriental character, is entirely the result of rebuilding after the great fire of 1906. When the Chinese invested in urban real estate, they adapted their cultural requirements to existing American architecture by the addition of elaborate balconies, paper or bronze lanterns, richly colored inscriptions, and rows of porcelain pots (Plate 46).

The British architects in California at mid-century were trained in the same "medieval" apprenticeships that distinguished their American colleagues, and their leader, William Patton, was both apprentice and associate to the famed Gothicist Sir Gilbert Scott. Like Patton, who arrived in San Francisco in 1849, the most prominent of the British architects came in the gold rush. These included William Crain, cofounder of the San Francisco Architectural Society, and David Farquharson, architect of such old San Francisco landmarks as the Cosmopolitan Hotel and the Bank of California (Plate 36). Patrick O'Connor served an apprenticeship in Birmingham, studied in Rome, and practiced briefly in Philadelphia prior to his arrival in San Francisco in 1852.

[9] The surviving joss house at Weaverville was not built until 1875. Alexander McLeod, *Pigtails and Gold Dust* (Caldwell, Idaho, 1947), p. 87; Will Oscar Upton, *Churches of El Dorado County, California* (Placerville, Calif., 1940), unnumbered photograph; *History of California*, ed. Zoeth Skinner Eldredge (New York, 1915), V, 475.

[10] William Henry Bishop, *Old Mexico and Her Lost Provinces* (New York, 1883), p. 374.

[11] Otheto Weston, *Mother Lode Album* (Stanford, 1948), pp. 90, 122, 160; *Alta California*, July 10, 1853; Barber and Baker, p. 101.

In 1855 an important Canadian immigration brought Samuel C. Bugbee and Joseph and Samuel Newsom to California. Bugbee won fame in the sixties and seventies as architect of the redwood palaces that housed Nob Hill's railroad and silver kings; the Newsoms succeeded not only as writers of architectural pattern books, but also designed what may be the finest surviving example of Victorian architecture in the United States—the Carson House at Eureka (Plates 50 and 51). Joseph Ough practiced in Pennsylvania and Ohio between his Canadian apprenticeship and settlement in Sacramento; Frank Walker arrived in California in 1864 at the age of twenty-one and began a career in Santa Barbara that threatened Peter Barber's long supremacy in that community.

Although German nationals were particularly active as builders in California in the late fifties, their representation among gold-rush architects is limited to John Apel and Victor Hoffman. Almost nothing is known of Apel, and even Hoffman, who acquired considerable fame after 1850 with the Mannerist Globe Hotel in Old Chinatown (Plate 27) and the Naglee Building, remains an enigma. By 1854, however, Henry Kenitzer of Baden had entered into his distinguished partnership with the pioneer architect David Farquharson, and in 1861 Jacob and Theodore Lenzen settled in San Jose and began constructing the first of many hundreds of buildings in the Santa Clara and San Joaquin valleys.

The French influenced the life and architecture of California in the last century to an extent that was out of all proportion to their actual numbers. According to the Census of 1850 French immigrants accounted for only 7 per cent of the foreign-born inhabitants, and by 1880 they ranked behind the Scandinavians. It is thought that in the early 1850's six thousand, or one half of the state's French population, resided in San Francisco—driven from the mines by a combination of Anglo-Saxon persecution and the cosmopolitan habits of a largely urban immigration. That they at once set about their business of building is evident from Frank Soulé's observation of 1854 that French "national taste and judicious criticism have virtually directed the more chaste architectural ornaments, both on the exterior and in the interior of our houses."[12]

[12] Page 463.

Nevertheless, only one French architect is positively known to have come to California in the great immigration. This is Prosper Huerne, who reached San Francisco in 1850 after graduating from the State School of Arts and Crafts at Châlons and serving with the government as a designer of provincial railway stations, bridges, and depots. Huerne drew upon this practical training not only in the execution of many early and important California commissions, such as the Bella Union gambling hall on Portsmouth Square and the Pacific Sugar Refinery, but also in his work as technical executor for the construction schemes of Ferdinand de Lesseps at the Isthmus of Panama.

Despite the lack of documentation regarding French architects on the California frontier, it is probable that both G. Morin Goustiaux and Emile Depierre came in the great immigration. Goustiaux is said to have lived in San Francisco as a boy and was probably the son of a pioneer manager of the *Franco Californien*. He returned to France, however, graduated from the Ecole des Beaux-Arts, represented the city of Paris at the World's Columbian Exposition in 1893, and, with William Mooser, designed the new French Hospital in San Francisco that same year. Of Goustiaux's colleague, Depierre, little is known other than that he graduated from the French Academy of Design and is said to have enjoyed a public and private practice in Paris before coming to the New World.

Peter Portois, the most celebrated European architect in California in the last century, emigrated from Belgium in 1851, spent several months in the mines, and returned to San Francisco that same year to design the Adelphi Theater—perhaps the first work wrought in the United States by a Beaux-Arts-trained architect, or at least so local tradition insists. For despite a fondness for discussing his student days at the Ecole, Portois is not listed by Edmond Delaire in *Les architectes élèves de l'Ecole des Beaux-Arts, 1793-1907* (Paris, 1907). This omission can be interpreted to mean that Portois did not pass into the higher classes, that he was not formally certified as a graduate, or that he was a liar. As contemporary sources list him as having attended the Ecole, conjecture is left to the reader.

The facts regarding the training of Albert Pissis at the Beaux-Arts are unequivocal. Furthermore, the Emporium and Hibernia Bank buildings (Plate 58) in San Francisco testify to his acquired academic tastes. Pissis came to California as a boy in 1858, graduated from the local schools, studied in Paris and Rome, and returned to San Francisco to become a leader in the western Neoclassic Revival on the Pacific frontier. He is the only known Mexican to practice architecture in California after the province became American.

Scandinavians assumed an importance as a regional minority in California in the late sixties and constructed some interesting wooden buildings along that part of the Mendocino coast where they settled as loggers and lumbermen. They are represented among architects in the great immigration by Augustus F. Eisen, a Swedish immigrant of 1854. A son, Theodore Eisen, educated in California schools and an architectural office in St. Louis, became one of Los Angeles' leading architects after 1870.

The biographer of the Swiss in California includes only one architect, a P. Righetti, among the large number of masons, stonecutters, and carpenters who emigrated from the Italian-speaking villages of the canton of Ticino.[13] His name and work, however, have escaped detection from any other source, and the houses that the Swiss erected in the Napa and Sonoma valleys suggest nothing of the architecture of their native canton. Further, the leading American-Swiss architect of the nineteenth century came from Geneva, and not the Ticino. This was William Mooser, cofounder of the San Francisco Architectural Society in 1861.

The significant factor in California history is the interaction of successive immigrant waves upon its life and culture. And nowhere is this so evident as in architecture. Until the gold rush the struggle for cultural supremacy was limited to the competing Spanish-Mexican and American colonial traditions. When the great immigration ended in 1869, however, California's population and architecture were truly international. The positive cultural achievements resulting from this heteroge-

[13] *The Swiss in the United States,* ed. John P. von Grueningen (Madison, 1940), pp. 97-98.

neous immigration are too often obscured by the racial and national animosities that accompanied them. The talent, training, and experience that the alien architects in the great immigration contributed to California's architectural frontier are, with the exception of Federalist Washington, historically and regionally unique. The discipline of the Ecole des Beaux-Arts, the precepts of the English masters, the competence of the German academies, together with the American classic tradition, merged in California after 1850 to produce a remarkable architectural renaissance.

IV. THE CALIFORNIA RENAISSANCE

THE COMING together of a score of cultures on a rich and isolated frontier produced the California Renaissance. The great immigration
furnished the human conditions; the wealth of mine, field, and factory
supplied the material means that made the several decades between the
gold rush and the railroad the most prosperous, progressive, and architecturally significant period in the nineteenth century. Though mining
was the state's largest employer of labor and capital, the feverish preoc-
cupation with gold lessened after the decline in placer production in
1853. With the return of the Argonauts to their historic trades and pro-
fessions, mills and factories sprang up in the burgeoning gold towns,
farms and vineyards spread over the mine-scarred foothills, and cattle
and sheep again roamed the unfenced southern ranges. Through all of
this period California continued its unique position as a sea frontier, developing an economy and culture largely outside of the national framework.

Excepting the mines and the remoter parts of the state, it was not
possible to build, plan, labor, or plant with any security of possession
until the question of the Spanish and Mexican land grants was at least
formally resolved. However, there seemed little possibility that Congress would feel bound by the assurances given at the time of annexation
that the United States government would respect the rights of landhold-

ers under provincial patents, for Americans had not seized California in order to protect the properties of several thousand Mexican citizens. The unprecedented immigration of '49 and '50, the demands of the miners for land indemnification, and Yankee hostility to Mexican custom and law determined the conditions of the Land Act of 1851, under which much of the property of the *Californianos* passed into the hands of the conquering foreigners. For if the United States Land Commission dealt expeditiously and fairly with most of the provincial grants, the partiality of the local courts and the right of repeated appeal by government attorneys and rival claimants subjected the patentees to such delay and expense that the end result was virtual confiscation. It is not surprising that the Montgomery Block, the finest building in the West in the mid-fifties, was constructed from legal fees earned in land cases.

Whatever the moral implications of the Land Act of 1851, its unrelenting application north of Monterey resulted in an unparalleled expansion in agriculture, industry, and building; conversely, the failure of the act to break up the colonial land grants in southern California assured economic and cultural stagnation. Less than 2 per cent of the 600,000 people who came in the great immigration settled in the southern counties. At a time when 2,500,000 acres of grazing land were reclaimed in northern California, and wheat production increased from 17,000 bushels in 1850 to 6,000,000 in 1860 and 16,000,000 in 1870, not 3 per cent of the acreage in Los Angeles County was under cultivation.

Cattle remained the principal industry of southern California. The demands for beef at the mines encouraged an enormous increase in native herds, and the introduction of shorthorn cattle from Kansas and Texas resulted in equally important stock improvements. This brief era of cattle prosperity, in which such inherited Andalusian practices as the rodeo, registered branding, and stock roundups were formally incorporated into California law, sustained a life of economic and social independence not unlike feudal Mexico. It also supplied the basis for that long-surviving pastoral legend that emerged in fiction as an idealized image of Spanish Colonial civilization. By 1872, however, the combination of drought and the Trespass Act destroyed the California cattle king-dom, opened up the range to settlement and farming, and doomed the rancho to mythology.

Despite the founding of progressive agricultural communities at El Monte, San Bernardino, and Anaheim, at no time in the nineteenth century were the northern and southern parts of the state so unequal in population, wealth, and achievement as in the years between the gold rush and the railroad. Not only did an inherited colonial land policy condemn the southern counties to economic and cultural backwardness through all of the "golden fifties," but even after the land problem was eased by the forced sale of Mexican estates following the famine of 1865, southern California was plagued by a chronic water shortage, primitive transportation, and a dearth of capital. When the great age of California building ended in 1869, there were only four architects registered south of San Jose, and Los Angeles, "queen city" of the cattle counties, was a sleepy Mexican village of yellow mud walls and dusty tar roofs—"an unsightly thorn in a surrounding patchwork of orange orchards and grape vineyards."[1]

Until the coming of the railroad in 1869, water transportation was the principal means of communication and traffic. This, together with the requirements of population, capital, and markets, forced the concen-tration of pioneer industry in the northern counties, and particularly in San Francisco, whose situation at the entrance to the great bay into which drain the river systems of the Sacramento and San Joaquin valleys assured its supremacy among western cities. At San Francisco, and at Sacramento and Benicia, tanneries were established as a by-product of the cattle industry. Here, too, the first mills were constructed to handle native and Australian wool. The state's several hundred flour mills were centered at Stockton, recently transformed from a secondary mining town into the principal city of the San Joaquin Valley. Raw cane sugar from Hawaii was refined locally, and iron ore, imported as ballast on the wheat ships, was converted at San Francisco and Sacramento into min-ing machinery, railroad equipment, and structural building materials.

By 1853 the architectural profession assumed a status and impor-

[1] Nadeau, *City-Makers* (New York, 1948), p. 3.

tance greatly superior to its earlier standing as a body of assemblers of tents, cabins, and imported New England frame buildings. In the score of years between the gold rush and the railroad, at least seventy-five architects came to California, almost all of whom settled in San Francisco, Sacramento, or San Jose. In 1861 the first architectural fraternity in the West was founded in San Francisco; in 1869 the California chapter of the American Institute of Architects was chartered.

Like builders everywhere in the United States in the last half of the nineteenth century, those on the California frontier relied heavily upon drawings, photographs, and pattern books for training and inspiration. And after 1852 architectural manuals were generally available. In March of that year Henry S. Fitch and Company sold a number of Richard Brown's *Domestic Architecture;* the *Alta California* reviewed Andrew Jackson Downing's *The Architecture of Country Houses* in January 1853 and recommended his designs as especially suitable because of the state's universal wood tradition. The bookseller George W. Murray opened his shop in the newly completed Montgomery Block in San Francisco in December 1853 with a substantial stock of architectural works, and his rivals, Le Count and Strong, advertised the books of Downing, John Bullock, and Henry Cleaveland with regularity in both the urban and rural press. Further, western students and apprentices were encouraged to use the well-stocked private libraries of the pioneer architects John Wright, Henry Cleaveland, and David Farquharson. Additional materials were available at the Mercantile Library and the Art Institute in San Francisco and the State Library at Sacramento.

The development of architectural construction after 1851 was as dramatic as the advances made in agriculture and milling. Instead of using costly imported materials as the forty-niners had generally done, the California builders now relied on native redwood, the production of which shifted under the insatiable demand from the Santa Cruz and Corte Madera groves to the vast stands of Mendocino, Humboldt, and Del Norte counties. That the wood building tradition brought from the East by successive waves of Yankee sealers, merchants, and gold seekers went unchallenged in domestic construction until the end of the century is uncontestable. The California houses, wrote a British traveler in the fifties, were "nearly all of wood, many of them well-finished two-storey houses, with columns and verandahs in front."[2] In the light of this, John Hittell's claim that three fourths of the state's dwellings in the sixties were of frame construction is an understatement.[3] By that decade more than 90 per cent of the buildings in San Francisco were frame structures and, excepting commercial blocks and factories, almost every building in the rural areas was wooden.

An important factor in making the frame house a commonplace on the California frontier was the introduction of the balloon frame into western building practices. This technique, which substituted nails for the traditional mortises and tenons and utilized light two-by-four-inch studs, took its name from the scorn in which it was held by conventional build-ers, who insisted that such frames would blow away "like balloons in the wind." As the finished house, covered with clapboards and roofed with shingles, was indistinguishable from the historic colonial model, it was widely accepted in California, where a shortage of skilled labor encour-aged any practical substitute for costly heavy-frame construction.

It is not known when the balloon frame became general in the West, but, as its use was dependent upon the manufacture of cheap machined nails, it was not widespread before 1849. Though it has been main-tained that the balloon frame was described in architectural pattern books only in 1865, and therefore not widely copied before the end of the Civil War, it is unlikely that San Francisco could have developed from a small village into a great city in a matter of months if gold-rush builders had been forced to rely wholly upon traditional heavy-frame construction. An article in the *California Architect and Building News* of June 1889, if inaccurate in describing the balloon frame as the "Cali-fornia style," is correct in reporting this technique in use on the coast during the four previous decades. A good example of balloon-frame construction from the late fifties is the row of houses at Westport, Men-docino County, illustrated in Plate 29.

[2] Borthwick, pp. 216-217.

[3] J. S. Hittell, *The Resources of California* (San Francisco, 1863), pp. 320-321.

Heavy fire losses in the gold communities encouraged large-scale production of bricks in San Francisco as early as 1849. But careless workmanship in mixing clay with salt water made these bricks inferior in quality to those burned in Sonora and at Shaw's Flat, where rich deposits of red lateritic earth assured first-grade bricks for the building projects of the Mother Lode country. Within several years, however, important manufacturing economies resulting from the introduction of mechanical devices, and the discovery of an adequate supply of limestone for mortar in the Sierra foothills and at Benicia, made brick second only to redwood as the state's building material. A single yard in Stockton turned out seven hundred thousand bricks in 1850; six years later a mechanical brick-making machine in San Francisco manufactured sixty thousand units a day; Los Angeles production reached two million per year by 1858.

The legendary granite walls of the Sierra Nevada notwithstanding, stone was hardly used in frontier California building. As late as 1869 only six of more than twenty thousand structures in San Francisco were of stone.[4] When granite was used in the early fifties, as in Parrott's Granite Block, it was generally imported from China because of the lack of a local extractive industry and the inadequacy of inland transportation. The stone for the foundation of Parrott's building, however, was quarried on Goat Island in San Francisco Bay, where in 1851 the New Englander Joseph Emery established a rubblestone works. Emery's product, a fine blue stone, was used in the construction of the San Francisco Navy Yards, Fort Winfield Scott, and the Bank of California (Plate 36). After completion of the Sacramento Valley Railroad in 1855, granite for northern California building was quarried principally at Folsom, twenty miles to the east of Sacramento.

In 1849 a Massachusetts farm boy, Calvin Nutting, founded the Pioneer Iron Works in San Francisco and turned out the first metal shutters and doors behind which California merchants sought to protect their property from fire and theft. Jonathan Kittredge opened the Phoe-

[4] Agnes Foster Buchanan, "Some Early Business Buildings of San Francisco, *Architectural Record,* XX (July 1906), 19.

nix Iron Works in the same year; the Eureka Iron and Brass Foundry of Sacramento advertised cast-iron shutters, capitals, building fronts, and stairsteps in 1856; and by 1869 more than seven iron foundries were in operation in San Francisco with an annual production in excess of $20,000,000. Examples of their work are the wrought-iron spiral staircases at Weaverville, Trinity County; the Greek Revival castings at Fort Winfield Scott; and the architectural iron work for Wright's Bank Building (Plate 19).

After 1853 structures not built of stone or brick were prohibited in the business districts of San Francisco, Sacramento, and Marysville; no other single fact testifies so dramatically and truthfully to the growth of permanent construction that accompanied the decline of placer mining. In 1854 there were five hundred fireproof buildings in Sacramento; the northern mining community of Shasta boasted the longest brick row in the West; and San Francisco, whose building area was extended by the reclamation of one hundred acres in the cove of Yerba Buena, raised fifteen hundred brick structures in the heart of its business area. The extent of the state's architectural self-sufficiency was the subject of an editorial in the *Alta California* of December 3, 1856, which noted that the recently completed Gibb Building in San Francisco had a basement of Angel Island stone, granite piers from the Folsom quarries, walls of locally fabricated brick, and a main doorway "ornamented and capped with very handsome free-stone, quarried near Benicia." The iron parts for this building were manufactured by Calvin Nutting, and the roof was of native asphalt.

The great immigration made California architecture cosmopolitan; it did not change its colonial character. Rather, it increased the number of competing colonial cultures to include every major European country. But while international rivalry was keen in civic and commercial building, the classic tradition established by Larkin and Colton predominated in domestic architecture during the period of the California architectural renaissance. This is true for both the metropolitan centers and the mining communities. In attributing the "glory and honor" of San Francisco to New England influences, the mayor declared in 1854 that the Yankee origin of his city could be seen everywhere, from its white frame houses to the spires of its churches and schoolhouses; a traveler at the mines in the same period wrote that with the exhaustion of the Sierra placers the "miserable little shanties or log cabins" were replaced with frame buildings of "unmistakably Yankee appearance, being all painted white turned up with green."[5] Here once again is demonstrated the utility of architecture in establishing the image of an age. For though the statistics of the great immigration establish conclusively the continuity in Yankee background of the Americans who came both before and after the gold rush, no testimony to California's New England heritage is more convincing than the spread of white-painted, green-shuttered frame houses over the San Francisco dunes and the Sierra foothills.

A photograph of the eastern slope of Nob Hill in San Francisco in 1856, reproduced in Plate 19, shows a number of typical Greek Revival frame houses of the gold era. Like most of the buildings discussed in this chapter, none of these have survived the changes of a century. And though the documentation for architecture in this period is admittedly incomplete, it nonetheless testifies to the Californians' penchant for classical forms in structures other than churches. This tradition in architecture was, after all, the only thing common to all of the competing colonial cultures. The Franciscan missionaries brought a Spanish edition of Vitruvius to Santa Barbara, the New England merchants carried the memory of Bulfinch's Boston to Monterey, and the British and French demonstrated their national interpretations of the Roman style in the great age of building that began in San Francisco in 1853. It is this universal commitment to the classical tradition that gives California's architectural frontier continuity and harmony despite the diversity in background and purpose of its builders.

Poor though they are, the Greek Revival cottages shown in Plate 19 suggest a striving for architectural refinement. Two of them, located just to the left of the upper floor of Wright's Bank Building and adorned with double galleries, French doors, and rudimentary Chippendale balustrades, were part of five such elevated houses that stood on Pine Street

[5] *Alta California*, Dec. 23, 1854; Borthwick, p. 101.

between Stockton and Dupont (Grant Avenue) in the mid-fifties. More impressive specimens of Greek Revival urban architecture are the Stanyon House, which according to an old sketch was embellished by an elliptical window cut under the portico roof; the Jerome Lincoln residence on Rincon Hill, said to have been distinguished by small paned windows, a spiral staircase, and a black and white marble sidewalk; and the Mission Dolores Parish House, whose shingled roof, green shutters, and fanlighted doorway typify the New England-oriented houses of the fifties (Plate 12).[6]

Captain John D. Sutter's "Hock Farm" on the Feather River near Marysville and the Phineas Banning Mansion at Wilmington testify to the widespread favor of Greek Revival forms in early California domestic architecture. "Hock Farm," pictured in contemporary photographs as a large two-story frame structure with double verandas, classical balustrades, and a handsome cupola, was set in a garden graced by lattice-work gazebos.[7] The Banning Mansion, constructed in 1864 after the manner of old houses that its builder remembered from his Delaware boyhood and described in 1870 as "probably the most commodious and homelike building in Los Angeles County," is the best extant example of Greek Revival domestic architecture in the state (Plate 33). Banning, developer of California's early stagelines, chief promoter of San Pedro harbor, and pioneer in the Los Angeles petroleum industry, was an exception to the tradition of the southern rancher—both in his devotion to industry and in his determination to have a house equal to any of his northern contemporaries.[8]

The publication of O. S. Fowler's *A House for All* in 1853 created a vogue for dwellings in the classical octagon form, which was not long in reaching California. The first of these experimental structures was the Los Angeles "Round House." Originally a circular dwelling, it was

[6] Watkins, *Builders of San Francisco*, p. 25; Mrs. Silas H. Palmer, *Vignettes of Early San Francisco Homes and Gardens* (San Francisco, 1935), pp. [5-6, 8].

[7] [Ida (Reyer) Pfeiffer], *A Lady's Visit to California, 1853* (Oakland, 1950), pl. facing p. 22.

[8] Marco R. Newmark, "Phineas Banning: Intrepid Pioneer," *HSSCQ*, XXXV (Sept. 1953), 268.

built of adobe materials by a French sailor who claimed to have modeled it after a house he had seen on the coast of Africa. About 1856 a later owner transformed it into an octagonal dwelling and enclosed the adobe walls within a clapboard frame. A photograph of Rincon Hill in San Francisco in 1856 shows a two-story structure obviously copied from the John J. Brown Octagon at Williamsburg, New York; however, in the California imitation the peaked roof of the original was replaced by a flat one. The Feusier Octagon, much altered but still standing on Russian Hill, was not only copied from one of Fowler's plans, but was constructed with the gravel and concrete walls that he insisted were both cheap and healthful.[9]

A copy of Fowler's book apparently fell into the hands of Henry Durant, first president of the University of California, for he called upon the well-known architect Henry Cleaveland in March 1860 with plans for an octagonal dwelling. Durant's unexecuted project, which followed Fowler's dictum regarding concrete walls and was somewhat originally distinguished by eight corner towers, was described by Cleaveland in a letter to his father as "the most ridiculous plan that ever came into the head of a noodle."[10]

The William G. McElroy House on Gough Street in San Francisco, restored in 1952 and presently state headquarters of the National Society of Colonial Dames of America, is the finest extant octagon in California. It was constructed almost one hundred years ago with walls made of a mixture of gravel and lime and finished on the outside with clapboards. The rooms are squared by the construction of closets in the corner angles; in the center of the house a circular stairway ascends from the first floor to the cupola. Like all of the octagons, the McElroy House affects Roman architectural forms in door- and window frames, wood-block quoins, and cornice.

Uniformity in style was the principal characteristic of California architecture in the fifties and sixties. In a land of cities this was inevitable, and by 1869 California was among the ten most urban states in the

[9] J. M. Guinn, "Historic Houses of Los Angeles," *HSSCQ*, III (1896), 68-69; George W. Hazard, "The Old Round House," *HSSCQ*, V (1901), 109-110; Watkins, pp. 16, 23-24.

[10] Mar. 26, 1860, Bancroft Library.

Union. That the inland towns exhibited the same conservative classical building standards as the coastal communities is illustrated in the print of Sonora made in 1853 by G. S. Wells, as well as in the Kuchel and Dresel lithograph of Nevada City engraved in 1856 and reproduced in Plate 24 and in photographs of the mining centers collected by the Historic American Buildings Survey. The Wells print, made at the height of placer activities, shows Sonora's Greek Revival Methodist Church, with steeple and slender pilasters, a number of story-and-a-half clapboard houses, and many framed and shuttered cottages scattered among the mounds of gravel, which were by-products of hydraulic mining methods. Plate 24 shows Nevada City in the mid-fifties, after successive fires had destroyed the frail and unseemly. Its principal churches are of the usual New England meetinghouse type; its major houses follow the Greek Revival academy style domesticated almost a decade before by Walter Colton at Monterey and Dr. Benjamin Shurtleff at Shasta (Plates 7 and 14). At the time Kuchel and Dresel engraved their famous lithographs of the Sierra towns, costly quartz mining methods had replaced crude placer techniques, trees were laid out along the straightened streets, and white-painted houses with green blinds and fanlighted doorways marked the advent of permanent village life in the diggings.

Numerous contemporary sources testify to the authenticity of the classic American frame cottage as the California archetypal house of the fifties and sixties (Plate 13). The dwellings of San Bernardino are described in an early history as wooden cottages, "painted white and half hidden in roses, jessamine, and honeysuckle"; the "Pioneer House" of the Anaheim colony, built about 1858, is a story-and-a-half dwelling with painted clapboards and the ubiquitous piazza.[11] There is a report of a farmhouse at San Juan Bautista in 1863 "reminiscent of Maine, with its white paint, green blinds and sharp gables"; another report describes the dwellings of San Jose—"as downright a little Yankee town as ever was"—as neatly painted frame houses behind picket fences.[12]

[11] History of San Diego County (San Francisco, 1883), p. 145; Hallock Floy Raup, The German Colonization of Anaheim (Berkeley, 1932), pls.

[12] Sarah Hathaway (Bixby) Smith, Adobe Days (Cedar Rapids, Iowa, 1925), p. 18; Taylor, Eldorado, p. 68; Bishop, p. 349.

Some existing examples of California houses from this period are the Grass Valley dwelling of Lola Montez, the two-story house of Major William Downie in Sierra County, and the frame cottages at Bridgeport.

Bodie, a restored ghost town on the eastern slopes of the Sierra Nevada in Mono County, is a single important exception to the characteristic California frontier mining community. Its period of greatest development (the late seventies), as well as its situation at an elevation of 8,500 feet amid barren wind-swept hills of sagebrush—"a land that God forgot"—suggests its affinity to the silver towns of Nevada and Colorado and the "Wild West" of Dodge City and Cheyenne. And like these towns, it had an unusually large number of bad men and a long record of gun fights and stage robberies. Though some of Bodie's buildings, such as the houses of Theodore Hoover and J. S. Cain, resemble the Yankee clapboard frames of Sonora and Angels Camp, most of them are poorly constructed of pine with false fronts of rough unpainted boards. Such typical frontier building, even if commonly portrayed in fiction and the motion pictures as the distinctive western vernacular architecture, was almost unknown in nineteenth-century California.

Brick was not favored in domestic building in the fifties and sixties because of the historic fear of earthquake, the mild climate, and the availability of redwood. When used, however, it attested to the wealth and importance of the house owner. The first brick dwelling in Los Angeles was a story-and-a-half structure erected in 1853 of materials kilned at the site by Captain Jesse Hunter, a veteran of the Mormon Battalion of 1846; a year later the "Antique Castle," the largest house in the state at the time, was constructed on the corner of Stockton and Sacramento streets in San Francisco of locally fabricated brick, plastered over and lined in imitation stonework.[13] Less flamboyant examples from the fifties are the two-story house put up in Santa Barbara by Captain Sparks; the surviving Whaley House in San Diego, with interior woodwork of eastern white cedar brought around Cape Horn; and the mansion William F. Walton built on Nob Hill in San Francisco in 1855,

[13] Newmark, *Sixty Years*, p. 115; San Francisco *Call*, Nov. 19, 1878.

"in the most approved modern style," at a cost of $10,000.[14] This house ultimately passed into the possession of William T. Coleman, the gold-rush builder turned capitalist who led San Francisco's Second Committee of Vigilance.

In 1858 the Sacramento architect Seth Babson designed for Shelton Fogus a brick house described in the local press as "the most perfect specimen of a residence in this State" (Plate 28). Plastered in buff-colored mastic, adorned with stone quoins, and admired at the time for its "chaste corinthian columns" and its "unique and faultless structure," it demonstrates the familiar American practice of disguising a typical colonial façade behind cumbersome French decorations. In 1861 the house was sold to the railroad builder and politician Leland Stanford, and it survives in greatly enlarged and altered form as an art gallery.[15]

Stone was used even less than brick in domestic building. One of the few examples from this period is the elaborate house in Gothic and Italian Villa styles designed by Thomas Boyd for John Marsh at the foot of Mount Diablo near Brentwood in 1856 (Plate 25). This existing country dwelling, constructed of cream-colored variegated stone quarried in the Contra Costa hills and of brick kilned on Marsh's own property, was lavishly praised in the contemporary press as "a most felicitous deviation from the prevailing style of rural architecture." Boyd's utilization of such unnecessarily heavy building materials was, however, rarely imitated because of the moderate climate and fear of earthquake —a fear justified by the destruction of Marsh's sixty-five-foot tower in 1868.[16] Some notable exceptions to this prejudice are the San Francisco Orphan Asylum, 1853-1854, constructed in the Gothic mode with dark sandstone quarried on the site; and a church and barn, apparently also in medieval style, built by J. M. Baldwin at Rockville, on the old road between Benicia and Sacramento.[17]

[14] *Alta California*, Nov. 3, 1855; Rensch, *Southern Counties*, p. 191; *Alta California*, Dec. 6, 1855; Scherer, *Coleman*, pp. 261-262.

[15] *California Farmer*, XVII (July 1862), 113.

[16] Parsons, *California Houses*, pp. 55-56; San Francisco *Daily Evening Bulletin*, July 19, 1856.

[17] *Crocker-Langley San Francisco Directory*, 1859 (San Francisco, 1859),

Despite the supremacy of the classical style in domestic architecture in this period, Gothic Revival houses were hardly a rarity. The most picturesque San Francisco dwelling of the mid-fifties was "Monroe's Medieval Mansion" on Russian Hill, said to have been constructed from a design by W. H. Ranlett out of materials shipped around South America from New England. Known as the House of Seven Gables, though there were actually eight of them, the Monroe Cottage had a square frame with four peaked roofs at the points of the compass and was one of the few consciously "quaint" houses of the gold era.[18] Other examples of pattern-book Gothic include a large frame dwelling in Sacramento, which Nathaniel Goodell designed and built in 1854 for his own use, and the country residence of Albert Dibblee in Ross Valley, Marin County (Plate 40). Goodell's house, with its large library, music room, and imported marble mantelpieces, testifies to the financial success of one of the pioneer members of the architectural profession in California. The Dibblee House, whose eastern origin is evident in the high-pitched roof and stylized decorations, may have been constructed from the designs of Henry Cleaveland, a leader in the California profession in the fifties and sixties.[19]

European interpretations of the classic tradition in domestic architecture became common in California with the return of the architects from the mines in 1853. Among the first of the imported styles to win general favor was the English Roman or Italianate, thought to have been introduced into the United States by Ammi Young, supervising architect for the Treasury Department and collaborator with Reuben Clark on the United States Marine Hospital at San Francisco in 1853. Be that as it may, the following year the severe classic spirit of Sir Charles Barry's Travellers' Club in London invaded San Francisco, and a number of buildings, all contemporaneous with South Park (Plate 21), were constructed in the classic style. South Park, the single California imita-

---

p. 10 (hereafter directories of this series cited as *San Francisco Directory*); Soulé, pp. 709, 716-717; Hoover, *Counties of the Coast Range*, pp. 624-625.

[18] Illustrated in Watkins, p. 20.

[19] Sacramento *Bee*, Jan. 4, 1950.

tion of a London crescent, was never completed, and the seventeen "stately brick residences" commented on in the 1854 Christmas edition of the *Alta California* disappeared in the fire of 1906. The project was developed by the Londoner George Gordon, who may have designed the first of the dwellings; Gordon Cummings, architect of the Montgomery Block, might equally well be responsible for the larger, flat-roofed houses of marked English style.

Despite the air of improvisation and unreality conveyed by Fardon's photograph, South Park was the setting for the first concentration of social wealth in San Francisco. In these two- and three-story houses, constructed of supposedly fireproof materials at a cost of $2,000, resided such prominent pioneer families as Gwin, Otis, Redington, Osgood, Haggins, and Tevis. By 1860, however, Rincon Hill, and then Nob Hill, overshadowed South Park, whose pathetic trees and barren paths contrasted grimly with the highly publicized hopes of the ambitiously conceived crescent.

Though the severe English Roman style of South Park continued to find favor as a domestic medium, California architects were more partial to the Italian Villa style—a less formal combination of round arches, pilasters, and entablatures—which at the time of the gold rush was popular in the East and won the approval of Andrew Jackson Downing. Indeed, it was Downing's friend and imitator, the pioneer architect Henry Cleaveland, who brought the Italian Villa form to the West Coast. It is not known when Cleaveland first used the style, but it was possibly introduced in the late fifties in the original design of the country house of William C. Ralston at Belmont in San Mateo County; and it is with the construction of country houses that the Italian Villa style is generally associated.

Country life developed early in California. On August 29, 1852, only two years after William Howard erected an imported frame house on his six-thousand-acre property in San Mateo County, an editorial in the *Alta California* claimed that almost every San Franciscan of means had an estate upon which he had built, or planned to build, a country house. Although this is certainly an exaggeration, the transformation of the San Francisco peninsula into the center for country life in the West was well under way by the time the San Bruno turnpike was finished in 1855. The completion of the San Francisco-San Jose railroad nine years later encouraged the planting of agricultural estates as far south as the Santa Clara Valley. It was in this latter period that Darius Ogden Mills laid out "Millbrae," near the present site of Burlingame, and commissioned Henry Cleaveland to design the most elaborate country house in the state. At the same time William Ralston, "the friend of every man in need," and the greatest patron of California architecture in the entire century, purchased the estate of Belmont and spent one million dollars in creating among its lime and ilex groves a showpiece of western horticulture and manufactures.[20]

Whatever the doubt regarding Cleaveland's connection with the original plans for the house at Belmont, it is known that he designed General John Bidwell's Chico Mansion in 1865 (Plate 34).[21] This house, still standing on the campus of Chico State College, is the representative example of the Italian Villa style on the Pacific frontier. More than that, it is the culmination of a quarter-century of building. A study of Bidwell and his dwellings during this twenty-five-year period reveals, in miniature, the history of the Americans in nineteenth-century California. Bidwell led the first party of overland farmers into the San Joaquin Valley in 1841 and constructed the first dwelling at the present site of Marysville; prospering as a farmer, he replaced this cabin with a house in the Monterey Colonial style made popular by his friend Thomas Larkin, and it was in this large, veranda-sheltered dwelling that he was living when the reports of gold reached him in March 1848. Within a month Bidwell was at the mines with a crew of Indian laborers, and, from wealth acquired in the Sierra and in subsequent business ventures, he hired Cleaveland to design his house in the latest of the styles domesticated on the California frontier.

The architecture of Second Empire France was introduced on the

[20] Julian Dana, *The Man Who Built San Francisco* (New York, 1936), pp. 170-171, 217; George Dunlap Lyman, *Ralston's Ring: California Plunders the Comstock Lode* (New York, 1937), pp. 98-99.

[21] Marcus Benjamin, *John Bidwell, Pioneer* (Washington, D.C., 1907), p. 33.

coast in the early fifties by a French consul, who erected an imported "Parisian" house near Portsmouth Square in San Francisco. This structure, described as having "double window-openings, small iron balconies on the first floor and a recessed doorway," is said to have been widely copied, and one imitation is illustrated in Plate 32, to the extreme right of the West End Hotel.[22] The trademark of the Second Empire style in domestic building was the mansard roof, which, supported by scroll-saw brackets and capped by a cast-iron cemeterylike fence, proved especially adaptable to western needs and was soon a commonplace in California urban architecture. It was in this tradition, known to the press of the sixties as the "modern style of architecture," that James and George Wolfe designed both the three-story San Francisco mansion of the historian Hubert Howe Bancroft and the recently razed Sutro House, built in 1863 for the proprietor of the Bella Union gambling hall. When Adolph Sutro bought the house with money earned in Nevada silver, he filled its extensive gardens overlooking the Pacific Ocean with a miscellany of Greek and Victorian statuary imported from Belgium and opened the grounds to the public as a promenade.[23]

As might be expected from the long classic tradition in American public building, the Greek and Roman derivative styles absolutely dominated civic architecture on the California frontier. This is evident in the design of the second San Francisco City Hall, constructed on the site of the old Parker House on Portsmouth Square in 1851 (Plate 15). Designed originally as a theater, and converted into municipal offices at great expense, the city hall was the first major piece of construction undertaken in California since the erection of Colton Hall in Old Monterey in 1847 (Plate 7). Whereas Colton Hall was designed in the simplest New England academy style, the city hall reflects, especially in its Doric pilasters and well-proportioned arches capped by sculptured keystones, the new architectural cosmopolitanism of the great immigration. Constructed of yellow sandstone imported from Australia, and originally unencumbered by the lantern or cupola shown in Fardon's photo-

[22] Ernest C. Peixotto, "Architecture in San Francisco," *Overland Monthly*, 2nd Ser., XXI (May 1893), 460.
[23] Palmer, pp. [27-28].

graph of 1856, the city hall is probably the work of Gordon Cummings, who is referred to as the designer of "most of the large edifices in the city" and is known to have designed the similar and adjoining Union Hotel.[24]

Testimony to the California preference for the classic style in civic architecture is available from every part of the state. The Mariposa County council, for example, resolved as a matter of course that their courthouse would be of "sturdy construction and classic design" and were rewarded with a structure "beautiful in its simplicity . . . built of hand-hewn timbers and whipsawed siding, held together with mortise, tenon, and wooden pegs."[25] Other specimens of civic architecture from the mines include the surviving Trinity County Courthouse at Weaver-ville, built about 1853 of brick overlaid with fitted stone; the IOOF Hall at Mokelumne Hill, Calaveras County, completed in 1856, of rhyolitic blocks; and the schoolhouse at Murphys, built in the same county several years later by volunteer labor (Plate 30).[26] One of the few examples of classic architecture from the southern counties is the first Los Angeles courthouse—a primitive, badly proportioned copy of Faneuil Hall in Boston by an architect presently known only as Deering. This structure, demolished in 1891, was accurately described in the seventies by a visiting Hapsburg grand duke as an architectural aberra-tion surmounted by a tower enclosing a noisy clock.[27]

The last important county building before the advent of the railroad was the Santa Clara County Courthouse in San Jose, built between 1866 and 1868 by the pioneer architect Levi Goodrich at a cost of almost $200,000, of which the designer is said to have realized a "pre-mium" of only $100. Goodrich, however, found compensation in his art. "Twice," recalls his biographer, "he visited the Old World to drink

[24] Soulé, p. 353; Idwal Jones, *Ark of Empire: San Francisco's Montgomery Block* (Garden City, N.Y., 1951), p. 59; *Alta California*, May 19, 1853.

[25] Weston, p. 3.

[26] *Alta California*, Oct. 27, 1856; Richard Coke Wood, *Murphys, Queen of the Sierra* (Angels Camp, Calif., 1948?), pp. 59-60.

[27] H. D. Barrows, "Recollections of the Old Court House and Its Builder," *HSSCQ*, III (1894), 40-42; Layne, "Annals of Los Angeles," Part II, *CHSQ*, XIII (Dec. 1934), 345.

in the genius that poised the dome of St. Peter, grained [groined] the arches of Cologne, or lifted up the spires of St. Paul." As would be expected of one to whom "the Corinthian capital, or Doric column, or Lombardian portico was a poem," Goodrich designed the courthouse in the "Roman Corinthian Order" and constructed it of sandstone from his own quarries south of San Jose. It is likely that the architect's son, E. B. Goodrich, who studied under his father and succeeded to his practice, also worked on the structure.[28]

The question of where the state would locate its legislature and public offices was contested between 1848 and 1853 by practically every California town except San Francisco. In 1849, after an uncomfortable session in the "unfinished box" provided by the city fathers of San Jose, the government alighted briefly at Vallejo, where the Mexican-American general of that name promised a $125,000 capitol building. This edifice, described by Bancroft as a "rather insignificant two-story building with a drinking-saloon and a skittle alley in the basement—the third house, as it was ironically called," was abandoned after one season. Next there was a session at Benicia in the surviving so-called Old California Capitol, a roomy, substantial brick building with a shingled roof and a Doric porch. Finally the legislature settled down at Sacramento in a handsome Greek Revival building with a full portico of ten Ionic columns designed by David Farquharson of San Francisco.[29]

In 1854 the legislature voted Sacramento the permanent seat of government and in 1856 broke ground for a state building. Lawsuits held up the project, and it was not until 1860 that seven architects submitted drawings and plans for a capitol, six of which were judged "fine specimens of architectural skill." Though the winning design has long dis-

[28] Frederic Hall, *The History of San José* (San Francisco, 1871), pp. 301-304; *Pen Pictures from the Garden of the World, or Santa Clara County, California*, ed. Horace S. Foote (Chicago, 1888), p. 226. This book also contains a fine picture of the courthouse, facing p. 139.

[29] As quoted in Writers' Program, *California's State Capitol* (Sacramento, 1942), pp. 30-33; *The Pioneer*, XIV (Dec. 1899), 145-146; the Old California Capitol at Benicia is one of the few California buildings cited in Talbot Faulkner Hamlin, *Greek Revival Architecture in America* (New York, 1944), p. 313 and Pl. XC; John Adam Hussey, "The Old State House at Benicia," *CHSQ*, XVII (Sept. 1938), 262-265.

appeared, and some doubt exists as to its true authorship, most sources agree that the original conception was the work of Miner F. Butler, architect of the State Agricultural Pavilion at Sacramento in 1859. However, the actual work of supervision was turned over to Reuben Clark, probably because of his experience in designing the Mississippi State Capitol. In 1866 Clark was judged insane, and Gordon Cummings took over the work. The building was officially occupied in 1869 and was completed five years later under the supervision of the state architect A. A. Bennett at a cost of more than one and one-half million dollars (Plate 31).[30]

Although the capitol was designed to be executed in solid granite blocks, only the ground floor was finished in stone before the lawmakers grew restive at mounting construction costs and ordered that the remaining work be carried out in brick and plaster. If its general form follows the example of the national capitol at Washington, the California Statehouse owes an obvious debt to the San Francisco customhouse for the arrangement of the porticos and for the rusticated façade of the ground floor. As a result of the prevailing taste for Roman architectural forms, and because of the constant change of architects, the original and simple classic design was submerged in a style not inaccurately described by a local chronicler as "florid Roman-Corinthian."[31]

In 1851 the United States Customhouse and Post Office was designed in Boston for erection in San Francisco (Plate 23). The work of Gridley Bryant, and known locally as the "Virginia Poorhouse" because of the number of southerners who sought employment within its chaste Greek Revival walls, the customhouse cost almost one-half million dollars to construct in 1855. An unusually large part of this sum went into foundations, which were secured only after an immense number of piles were driven into the marshy site and a massive base of granite was laid down to support the brick edifice. Described in the local press

[30] Writers' Program, *State Capitol*, pp. 40-47; Sacramento *Daily Union*, May 21, 1860; Thompson & West, *History of Sacramento County, California* (Oakland, 1880), pp. 91-92; *Alta California*, Aug. 22, 1860; *Sacramento Directory*, 1870, p. 173.

[31] William Ladd Willis, *History of Sacramento County, California* (Los Angeles, 1913), p. 363.

as "doric" in style and "by far the handsomest building in California," the customhouse was designed in the tradition of Robert Mills's post of-fice building in Washington and was the first example of the monumen-tal federal office building on the Pacific Coast.[32]

The last important Greek Revival structure in California, and by all standards the most magnificent, is the extant United States Branch Mint at San Francisco, begun in 1869 and finished in 1874 (Plate 39). The architect, Alfred B. Mullett, like so many of California's own practi-tioners, was born in England and came to the United States at an early age. He was appointed supervising architect of the Treasury Depart-ment in 1866, and the San Francisco mint was his first government commission. Executed in blue-gray stone over brick, with six mono-lithic sandstone columns supporting a portico, the mint relies upon plain, square pilasters and a splendid Doric frieze for ornamentation.[33]

Talbot Hamlin called the San Francisco mint a monument to the spirit of the Greek Revival brought west by American immigrants.[34] Pleasant as it would be to claim the mint as an indigenous production, it is merely another example of architectural colonialism. Mullett, like Colton in the pioneer period and Bryant in the gold era, designed his structure without regard for western taste or regional conditions. Con-sidering this, it is not strange that so magnificent a building was thought incongruous even in architecturally rich San Francisco, and that a con-temporary observer described its columns, "like fluted and petrified pines," as contrasting "too violently with the light and uncertain archi-tecture of a city of wood."[35]

If the Gothic Revival met with only indifferent success in domestic architecture, and none at all in civic and academic, it was supreme in

[32] Continuation of the Annals of San Francisco, comp. Dorothy Huggins (San Francisco, 1939), pp. 34, 69; William A. Newman, "Development of Federal Architecture in California," Architect and Engineer, LIV (July 1918), 67; Ham-lin, pp. 313-314; Alta California, May 31, 1854; Jan. 21, Oct. 6, 1855.

[33] Hamlin, p. 314; The National Cyclopædia of American Biography, XXVII (New York, 1939), 452.

[34] Page 314.

[35] Benjamin E. Lloyd, Lights and Shades in San Francisco (San Francisco, 1876), p. 397; Benjamin Franklin Taylor, Between the Gates (Chicago, 1880), p. 174.

California church construction. The transition from the classical meet-inghouses of the gold rush to the medieval churches of the silver decade was made in 1852 when the Methodist-Episcopal body of San Fran-cisco replaced their imported frame with a substantial board-and-batten structure in the "perpendicular style" that is possibly the work of Louis R. Townsend (Plate 16). Soon congregations throughout the state were recasting the New England timbered church in brick in the Gothic tradition. The First Congregational Church in Sacramento, de-signed by Albion Sweetser in 1854, is typical of these crude "castel-lated" structures whose towers and ropework scarcely concealed a con-ventional model and method of construction (Plate 20). Some surviv-ing examples from this period are St. James's at Sonora, built in 1859 from the plan of its pastor, John G. Gassman, and old St. Mary's in San Francisco, designed by William Crain and Thomas England in 1853.[36]

None of the less conventional double-towered churches of the sixties are extant. Some of them, however, were important, and one at least— the Roman Catholic St. Francis' Church—was copied from St. Patrick's Cathedral in New York. At the time of its completion in 1860, St. Francis' is said to have been the only "legitimate" western example of a church with a two-towered façade of medieval design.[37] Another, San Francisco's famous second Temple Emanu-El (Plate 35), designed by William Patton in 1865 in the "Gothic Byzantine" tradition, was the model for all subsequent temple construction in California.[38] The last important Gothic church before the arrival of the Pacific railroad was the Starr King Chapel (Unitarian), designed by Patton in 1864 just prior to the death of the famous California preacher and Unionist for whom it was named. This structure, considered at the time a marvel of flamboy-ant fifteenth-century style, has long since disappeared. Its loss is not an architectural calamity.[39]

[36] *San Francisco Directory*, 1858, p. 374; *California Farmer*, Nov. 16, 1854, p. 154; Sacramento *Union* (Pictorial Edition), Jan. 1855; Weston, p. 50; *San Francisco Almanac for the Year 1859* (San Francisco, 1858), p. 76.

[37] *San Francisco Almanac 1859*, p. 78; Lyle F. Perusse, "The Gothic Revival in California, 1850-1890," *Journal of the Society of Architectural Historians*, XIV (Oct. 1955), 18-19.

[38] *San Francisco Directory*, 1866, p. 15.

[39] Ibid., 1863, pp. 503-504.

The French traveler Ernest de Massey, writing to his cousin from San Francisco in 1850 about the recurring fires in the gold communities, advised that no California property would be secure until regional architects began to build in brick and stone, "a matter of many more years."[40] Scarcely thirty months after this pessimistic report there were more than one thousand fireproof buildings in northern California alone, and the state's pioneer historian could declare that the era of tents and shanties had passed into one of brick and granite.[41] The measures taken to protect property against fire and flood losses, such as granite foundations, solid walls of brick two to three feet thick, and double doors and shutters of wrought iron, endowed early industrial and commercial building with a fortresslike massiveness that struck contemporary visitors as both unique and splendid.

One of the earliest metropolitan examples of fireproof construction is the extremely utilitarian building erected on Portsmouth Square in the summer of 1851 to house the gambling facilities of the El Dorado (Plate 15). Almost certainly the work of the French-trained Prosper Huerne, who is known to have designed the rival Bella Union about the same time, the El Dorado hall is typical of the severe fire-resistant construction of the early fifties. Huerne's work, which usually followed the style of the factory shown in the extreme right of Plate 22, included the Pacific Sugar Refinery, the North Point Docks, and possibly the Pacific Rolling Mills and the Mission Woolen Mills of San Francisco.

A surprisingly large number of San Francisco's brick and stone structures were architecturally important and, according to a local historian, "were better designed and better looking than those used for like purposes anywhere else in the United States at that time."[42] Perhaps the earliest of these was the building erected on the southwest corner of Montgomery and Merchant streets in 1850-1851 by the merchant Henry Naglee, whose previous place of business had been consumed by

[40] "A Frenchman in the Gold Rush," trans. and ed. Marguerite (Eyre) Wilbur, *CHSQ*, V (Mar. 1926), 26.

[41] Soulé, pp. 492-493; *Sacramento Directory*, 1854-1855, pp. 5-6; Bancroft, *History of California*, VI, 776.

[42] John Philip Young, *San Francisco: A History of the Pacific Coast Metropolis* (San Francisco, 1912), I, 143.

fire four times in less than one year. A small brick structure embellished with eighteenth-century French details in stone and wrought-iron balconies, the Naglee Building was described by one critic as "a very respectable piece of mid-century Parisian design." Possibly the work of Victor Hoffman, it demonstrates some kinship to the Globe Hotel (Plate 27), which the enigmatic architect built in San Francisco's Old Chinatown in 1857.[43]

The Globe Hotel is one of the consciously Mannerist productions of the California Renaissance. Although the photograph reproduced in Plate 27 shows the building after its conversion to warehouse and office use in the late nineteenth century, the beautiful proportions and superb stuccowork are still evident. The capricious ornamentation of the window frames in the second and third stories recalls Viennese palace architecture and hints that Hoffman may have emigrated from the old Hapsburg empire. The extraordinary quality of the stuccowork suggests the talents of two little-known pioneer architectural plasterers, Carpeaux and Pepin, the latter of whom is said to have won a first prize at the University of Paris for excellence in design and execution of his art.[44]

Most hotel construction on the California frontier after 1855 followed the severe English Roman style popularized by A. A. Bennett in the Golden Eagle at Sacramento and Thomas Boyd in his designs for the International Hotel and the Railroad House in San Francisco. In these buildings the architects forsook the Greek Revival forms so familiar in such gold-era hostelries as the Parker House, Oso at Bear Valley, and the Eureka (now St. George) at Volcano for quoins, pilasters, and arches painted dark against light-colored stucco walls. The apogee of the style was reached by Johnston and Mooser in 1861-1862 with the Occidental Hotel and the Russ House, both built in San Francisco of brick covered with plaster painted in contrasting shades of cream and brown.[45]

The life and atmosphere of the great hotels of the sixties apparently underwent a transformation as dramatic as their style transition from

[43] Ibid.; Buchanan, "Business Buildings of San Francisco," pp. 23-25.
[44] "A Frenchman in the Gold Rush," p. 20.
[45] Sacramento County and Its Resources (Sacramento, 1894), pp. 134-135; Soulé, pp. 650-651; Alta California, Oct. 15, 1854; Weston, p. 118.

Greek Revival to English Roman. For suddenly respectability became the rule. This is evident in the beautiful banquet hall of the Lick House, whose designer entirely eschewed the nudes so beloved by the forty-niners and hung his classic walls with heroic paintings of California scenes by Thomas Hill and William Keith (Plate 37). Under the same influence, the proprietor of the famous gentleman's bar in the Montgomery Block discreetly redecorated that establishment with "choice" engravings of the French Revolution. And, to the shame of the bad old days of the gold rush, the Occidental, where Emerson stayed in 1871, is said to have become as genteel as any contemporary Boston hotel. However, occasional reports of life as actually lived in these great hotels, and especially in those bordering on the Barbary Coast, suggest that this shift to gentility may have been more of a surface change than a genuine moral revolution. An example of the unreliability of San Francisco appearances is the collapse of part of the Occidental in 1861, despite its seeming solidity.

The state's first major commercial building, Parrott's Granite Block, was designed by the pioneer architect Stephen Williams and built in San Francisco in 1852 at a cost of $117,000. In his specifications Williams followed faithfully John Parrott's insistence upon a basement of stone embedded in cement, a superstructure of twenty-inch brick walls, and the protection of all openings by doors and shutters of one-quarter-inch cast iron. The granite used in this structure was imported from China; the labor connected with its construction was performed by Chinese coolies brought to San Francisco to work from sunrise to sunset for a daily wage of one dollar and a ration of rice and fish. In the absence of derricks, the workers utilized bamboo poles along which they pushed the heavy granite blocks. The style, described at the time as "Georgian," was dependent upon flattened Italianate arches, a classic pediment, and bracketed window hoods. Parrott was so pleased with the finished building that he presented the architect with a horse and buggy as a bonus—a gesture that Williams refused, regarding the gift as a breach of the ethical code of the nineteenth-century practitioner.[46]

[46] Buchanan, pp. 20-23; letter of John Parrott to the Hon. T. Buller King, San

The style of Parrott's Granite Block was only occasionally imitated by commercial builders in California at mid-century. The beautifully dressed and fitted stone building that housed the Prince and Garibaldi Store at Angels Camp is one of the few surviving specimens from the mines; the Pico House on the old Plaza at Los Angeles, though designed a decade later, is another extant example (Plate 38). Long the finest building south of San Jose, the Pico House was designed by Ezra Keysor and Octavius Morgan for the former Mexican governor Pío Pico, and was the first three-story structure in Los Angeles.[47]

The mining communities followed the architectural lead of San Francisco in the construction of fireproof buildings, and restored Columbia, widely advertised as a gold-rush town despite the fact that none of its surviving buildings antedate the disastrous fire of July 10, 1854, is the best example of this early stage of permanent brick construction. Although Columbia's two-story asphalt-roofed buildings are more picturesque than significant, sometimes, as in the cast-iron balcony railings and ornamental brick cornices, attention was given to architectural refinement. And if poorly constructed, the brick structures were carefully designed and had excellent drawings and specifications. One of these structures, the Wells, Fargo and Company Building, constructed according to its original contract in 1858, has handsome iron grills ordered in Troy, New York, and hauled to Columbia by mule freight.[48]

With the building of the Montgomery Block in San Francisco in 1853, California commercial architecture came of age (Plate 18). The work of the English-trained Gordon P. Cummings, this structure was the most important piece of regional architecture of the mid-fifties. It was constructed at a cost variously estimated from six hundred thousand to several millions for Captain Henry W. Halleck, a member of a prominent pioneer law firm and later commander-in-chief of the Union armies. Halleck, trained at West Point as a civil engineer in military for-

---

Francisco, May 2, 1852, in the California Historical Society Collection; undated letter of Williams' granddaughter, Mrs. Jannopolis, to the author.

[47] Newmark, *Sixty Years*, p. 396.

[48] Francis W. Wilson, "A Preliminary Architectural Study of the Old Mining Town of Columbia" (mimeographed at Berkeley, 1936), pp. 21, 42; Weston, p. 56.

tifications, was responsible for the redwood-log base upon which the structure rests; apparently he also suggested the building's basic architectural style. His drawings for an interior court in the Renaissance tradition, however, were scrapped by Cummings in favor of a glazed, London-type areaway planted with boxed greenery.[49]

In discussing the Montgomery Block in an interview reported in the San Francisco *Daily Herald* of December 23, 1853, the architect declared that "in extent, permanency of construction, and architectural beauty," his building would claim more than ordinary attention in any part of the world. In the West, of course, it was without a rival. Like most of the commercial developments in California in the second half of the last century, the Montgomery Block was constructed of brick, covered with plaster, and roofed with a combination of cement and asphalt. The provision of diagonal iron ties as resistance against earthquake torque is considered by critics as a notable innovation. The base course of the building is a gray granite; the stone used for the sills and keystone sculptures is ocher in color and poor in quality.

The architect worked twenty-eight shops into a ground-floor arcade of rectangular stone piers and surmounted this by three stories in the restrained Italian manner of contemporary English urban models. The fenestration of these upper stories is especially distinguished and conveys a striking sense of modernity by its economy of detail and dramatic contrast between relief molding and recessed aperture. Although these features are the best part of the building, Cummings, in the newspaper interview quoted above, generously allowed that the *"chef d'oeuvre* of the whole edifice" was the sculptured stonework of the Montgomery Street façade. This was the work of California artists and included a bust of Washington over the bronze entrance doors, columns "in alto-relievo ... from the style of the Diocletian baths at Rome," and, serving as keystones for the arches of the store fronts, the sculptured heads of Franklin, Jackson, Clay, the architect, the builder, the sculptor, and the collector of the port of San Francisco.

[49] Buchanan, pp. 25-26; George Tays, "The Montgomery Block," MS in the Bancroft Library; Young, I, 143; Jones, pp. 38, 61, 66.

The destruction of the Montgomery Block in 1959 removed the last significant link with San Francisco's frontier past. No other building represented so well the color, drama, and achievement of the several decades that make up the period of the California Renaissance. Here were the offices of the state's leading lawyers and engineers, its editors and politicians. In the Merchant Street wing, occupied by Adams Express Company, much of the gold brought from the Sierra was stored and minted; in the second-floor lobby above the Bank Exchange Bar much of California's commercial and political business was transacted. In the bar itself San Francisco's legendary "Pisco Punch" was dispensed without interruption until the sad days of prohibition. It was from his office in this famous building that the crusading editor, James King of William, stepped onto Montgomery Street one evening in June 1855 and was shot down by James P. Casey. This event provoked the calling of the Second Vigilance Committee, and the Montgomery Block served as one of its headquarters. Even after the Civil War, when its material fortune declined, the block remained pre-eminent as the center for San Francisco's much-publicized literary and Bohemian life.

In 1854 Peter Portois designed a bank for erection on the corner of Montgomery and Jackson streets that threw all the post-Montgomery Block buildings into architectural obscurity. The last major piece of construction before the depression of 1853-1854 forced a brief cessation of building, Wright's Bank Building followed the usual California tradition of a first floor of cut granite and a superstructure of hard-burned brick bound with iron and plastered in simulated stonework (Plate 19). This "extremely competent bit of Parisian architecture of the period of the third Napoleon," with its rusticated ground story, confusion of classic pediments, continuous balconies, heavily bracketed cornice, and elaborate lantern, sums up the transition from an older Greek Revival tradition to an emerging Beaux-Arts dictatorship.[50]

Portois, who was fond of boasting that he was really the leading architect of Belgium, selected the site adjoining Wright's Bank Building for the construction of his masterpiece: the Hibernia Society and Bank Building (Plate 26). This structure, finished in 1857, and the first of a

[50] California Farmer, Dec. 28, 1854, p. 202; Buchanan, pp. 29-30.

long and celebrated series of "American Renaissance" productions, is the Beaux-Arts prototype in California. Though there exists some doubt regarding Portois' European training, and therefore his right to claim the distinction of being the first graduate of the Ecole to practice in the United States, Portois' work establishes him as the progenitor of that immense architectural effort usually thought to have begun with Richard Morris Hunt's New York commissions of the 1880's.[51]

In the design for the Hibernia Society and Bank Building, Portois confined his talent to the interpretation of well-established classic forms, especially the palace architecture of Verona and Vicenza. Such discipline was all too rare, and in his later San Francisco commissions, particularly the West End Hotel (Plate 32), Portois demonstrated his preference for Venetian-Victorian forms. The scheme for the Hibernia project is typically eclectic in its Palladian balance and utilization of the Corinthian order for column and pilaster. Though the photograph reproduced in Plate 26 was taken almost fifty years after the building was finished and shows the hard use to which the structure was put, the splendid stuccowork distinctive of the California Renaissance is very much in evidence. It is interesting to note that the structure McKim, Mead and White designed for the Century Club in New York in 1891 is extraordinarily similar to this San Francisco clubhouse and bank of the gold era. Whether or not Stanford White was familiar with the bank is a matter of conjecture; it is enough to observe that Portois brought the neoclassic movement in the United States to a modest flowering on the California frontier some three decades before the so-called renaissance of McKim, Mead and White.

Seven years after James Bogardus erected the first American cast-iron building in New York City in 1848, a similar structure was reported in San Francisco—a three-story brick and mastic building with "tasty" cast-iron columns and large expanses of plate glass. In 1856 a two-story iron structure was constructed on Sansome Street in the same city, and in the following year Thomas Boyd designed a like building, "in the Corinthian style of architecture, painted and bronzed," of materials cast locally by the Sutter Iron Works. None of these edifices, however, ex-

[51] Buchanan, pp. 28-29.

hibited any originality in construction or design. The only known case where the architects of cast-iron structures gave serious concern to regional conditions was the Bank of British North America, in the construction of which Wright and Sanders anchored their iron frame to an inner wood support designed to take the shock of earthquake.[52]

In the 1860's iron cagelike buildings with sheets of plate glass and rows of stamped decorations were everywhere met with in San Francisco, Sacramento, San Jose, and Marysville. Their façades, with a wild profusion of Palladian motifs, Corinthian capitals, and elaborate quoins, show an unfortunate zeal in putting to the ultimate test Bogardus' boast of the "happy adaptability" of cast iron to stamped ornamentation. Typical of these, and the largest iron building in the state at the time, was S. H. Williams' New Merchants' Exchange on California Street in San Francisco, reported in the contemporary press as boasting a first story of "pure Doric" style, a second of "Ionic derivation," a third of "highly ornamented Corinthian," and finally an attic described as "modernized medieval." Each story was recessed ten feet to form a balustrade and carried an additional weight of colossal "cyclopian Etruscan" vases.[53]

In 1864 William C. Ralston launched the Bank of California with a capitalization of $2,000,000 and hired David Farquharson to design a structure suitable for the greatest banking house in the West. Two years later a replica of Sansovino's Library of St. Mark was reared on Sansome Street in San Francisco, and even Mark Twain was impressed (Plate 36). Ralston's bank was the last monument of the California Renaissance and one of the few commercial buildings constructed after 1852 in solid stone. Each of the bank's forty-two columns was a single block weighing from three to four tons; the interior was finished in Spanish mahogany and black marble. The scene of a disastrous currency run during the panic of 1875, and long one of the principal buildings on the Pacific Coast, the Bank of California vanished, along with its age, in the fire of 1906.[54]

[52] *Alta California*, July 12, 1855; June 12, 1857; *San Francisco Directory*, 1867, p. 13.

[53] *San Francisco Directory*, 1868, pp. 13-14.

[54] Bishop, p. 304.

Scarcely a building survives as testimony to the California Renais-sance, the brilliant score of years between the gold rush and the coming of the railroad. And though architecture gives perhaps the most truthful picture of that unique frontier society described by Walt Whitman as "fresh come to a new world indeed, yet long prepared," the splendid buildings of the fifties and sixties were almost wholly unknown outside of the state at the time of their construction and have only now found their biographer.

Yet nowhere in history is there so extraordinary an example of archi-tectural growth or so dramatic an exception to the usual criteria of the frontier as the California cities in the decades between the gold rush and the railroad. The explanation for the singular importance of architecture in this period lies not alone in Sierra gold and Washoe silver, for, as the typical mining frontier proves, sudden mineral wealth more often than not is productive of only a wild and brief extravagance. Equally essential to an understanding of the California Renaissance is the nature of the great immigration and the extreme physical isolation that forced the Cal-ifornians to create out of their own resources a unique colonial culture. Dixon Wecter understood this when he wrote, "Unlike earlier frontiers, that of northern California enjoyed both the wealth to patronize art and the cosmopolitan spirit to create it."[55] It was inevitable that in a new, rich, progressive, and international society important architectural ad-vances would take place. That California anticipated by three decades the American Classic Renaissance was one of the cultural compensations for the turbulence, disappointment, and waste of the gold rush.

[55] "Instruments of Culture on the Frontier," *Yale Review*, XXXVI (Winter, 1947), 254.

V. A CYCLE OF REVIVALS

I N MAY 1869 the Pacific railroad reached California and ended one
hundred years of historic isolation. For the first time Californians regarded themselves as part of the Union they had helped to preserve. As
an editorial in the *Alta California* of May 10 put it, "California was formally admitted by an act of Congress to the sisterhood of states nineteen
years ago but that relation did not become a real, visible, tangible fact
till the last rail was laid." But if the state was no longer a maritime colony
of the United States, the physical fact of the frontier remained. There
were still scarcely three inhabitants for every square mile of territory, and
excepting several thousand Mexicans practically every adult in California was born outside the state—and almost 40 per cent were born
outside the Union. As immigration remained the major source for population growth and the accretion of talent, architecture continued to be
predominantly colonial.

The coming of the railroad coincided with the passing of the pioneer
phase of frontier exploitation and the beginning of a long period of political corruption and economic depression. Shortly after the arrival of the
railroad, the discovery of the richest vein in the Comstock lode launched
a few years of feverish mineral exploitation. However, the Big Bonanza
only superficially resembled the great days of '49, when gold stimulated

everything from agriculture to architecture, and it contributed little to the state's permanent well-being. The frenzied interlude of Nevada silver speculation in the early seventies did stave off temporarily the effects of the national panic of 1873. But the end result was to make even more calamitous the crash that followed the failure of the Bank of California in 1875. And excepting the factories, banks, theaters, and hotels that sprang from the ambitions of William Ralston, the building projects of the silver kings were crude and bizarre examples of conspicuous waste.

Though it was difficult during this period of economic depression to secure sufficient capital for the development of the state's agricultural and industrial resources and the promotion of necessary architectural construction, it seemed for a brief period in the eighties as if Los Angeles might duplicate the dramatic growth in farming, industry, and building that distinguished the northern counties in the decades following the gold rush. In 1870 Los Angeles had fewer than 6,000 people, and land sold for under three dollars an acre; in 1887 its population was nearly 100,000, and property values had risen sixty million dollars. In the latter year the Santa Fe Railroad reached the southern capital, and its owners, taking note of a land subsidy of ten million acres, promoted the land rush of 1887. In less than a year the Santa Fe was selling one-way tickets from Kansas City for a low of one dollar, whole counties in the Midwest were depopulated, and sixty new communities were raised upon the ruins of the ranchos.

But the land bubble burst within a year, and many of the brilliantly advertised communities—including Santa Monica, "Zenith City of the Sunset Sea"—were deserted. Nonetheless, this period brought revolutionary changes to every part of southern California. In 1870 a citrus grove was spoken of as a curiosity, and the petroleum industry was limited to the production of asphalt roofing materials; in 1888 there were 2,000,000 bearing orange trees, and the annual production of oil was 700,000 barrels. The most significant changes, however, were in the nature of the population. For the land rush buried the Spanish-Mexicans in an avalanche of Anglo-Saxon immigrants and made Los Angeles the only county in the state inhabited largely by Americans.

For all of this, the amount of architectural construction at the end of the century was less than at any time in the prosperous decades following the gold rush. In desperation at declining employment and wages, the California workingmen turned upon the Chinese—some fifteen thousand of whom were thrown into the labor market upon the completion of the railroad. After reaching its peak in the Pullman riots at Sacramento, Oakland, and Los Angeles, railroad-union violence spilled over into the building trades in a series of bitter disputes that continued until the renewal of construction in San Francisco following the fire of 1906. The growing body of architects, hit harder by the continuing cycle of depression than any other group, vainly sought to enforce a 5 per cent professional fee and to limit the practice of architecture through municipal and state regulation. The desperate state of building at the close of the century is testified to by the replacement of professional notices in the pages of the *California Architect and Building News* with advertisements guaranteeing immediate profits to those undertaking the art of taxidermy.

Though the population gains made in the years subsequent to 1869 were less than those of the preceding several decades, the tradition of California immigration—reinforced by the land rush of the eighties and the building opportunities resulting from the long-delayed development of the southern counties—attracted a body of architects to California second in importance only to those of the great immigration. As was traditional, the largest number of American builders who came west with the railroad were from New England and New York. Chief among these was Bernard Maybeck, a graduate of the Ecole des Beaux-Arts, recipient of the Gold Medal of the American Institute of Architects, and creator of the Bay Area style. Others were J. A. Walls, who joined the pioneer Los Angeles firm of Keysor and Morgan in 1888 after three years in the Boston office of Henry Hobson Richardson; Sumner P. Hunt, the leading exponent of the Mediterranean style on the coast; and A. Page Brown, the foremost architect in San Francisco in the late eighties and at one time an associate of McKim, Mead and White. This celebrated eastern firm also trained John Galen Howard, a graduate of

Massachusetts Institute of Technology and founder of the school of architecture at the University of California.

Fewer architects born and trained in the British Empire took part in the southern California real estate boom than participated in the gold rush. However, their numbers included such important designers as William Weeks, president of the southern chapter of the American Institute of Architects, and James Reid, graduate of McGill University, student at the Beaux-Arts, and architect of the surviving Hotel Del Coronado. Among those immigrating to San Francisco in the same period were William Curlett and Harold Mitchell, both trained at the Art Institute of Manchester, and Ernest Coxhead, a graduate of the school conducted by the Royal Institute of British Architects in London. Augustus Laver, who was to win fame and abuse as the architect of San Francisco's third city hall, arrived in California in 1870 after a celebrated London, Canadian, and American practice, which included designs for the parliament buildings at Ottawa, the Bank of British North America at Quebec, the remodeling of the Roman Catholic cathedral in Montreal, and, with Thomas Fuller, the New York capitol at Albany.

The location of the main offices of the California Immigrant Union at Hamburg and Bremen had a significant effect on architecture, and Germans made up the largest single foreign-born element in the immigration of the eighties. A leader in this second wave of Germans was August Wackerbarth, who arrived in Los Angeles in 1882 and helped found the local architectural society. Others were the Heidelberg-educated C. J. Kubach; Wildrich Winterhalter, who dotted northern California with breweries and malt houses; the former government architect Edmund Kollofrath, author of many factories and commercial buildings in San Francisco, Santa Cruz, Chico, and Redwood City; and Harry Blackman, a student at the Royal Academy of Architects in Berlin, chief architect for the government of Victoria, Australia, and designer of the International Exposition at Sydney in 1879. A fellow of both the Royal Academy and the Royal Society of Architects, Blackman came to Los Angeles for health reasons in 1886.

At the time of the Los Angeles building boom, San Francisco architects dominated the western profession. Their unofficial organ, the *California Architect and Building News*, was founded in 1880 in imitation of the *American Architect and Building News*, whose drawings and photographs the western journal freely copied. About 1883 the San Francisco chapter of the American Institute of Architects initiated the first classes in design on the West Coast, and even though these were conducted in the rarefied atmosphere of the Ecole des Beaux-Arts, they at least served to introduce a number of young men to freehand drawing, modeling, and "practical architecture." This program was absorbed in 1893 by the San Francisco Art Institute, at that time quartered in the Mark Hopkins Mansion on Nob Hill and distinguished by the presence of Bernard Maybeck. Additional instruction in architecture was available at the Mechanics' Institute, the Van der Naillen School of Engineering in San Francisco, and the California Military Academy in Oakland.[1]

Despite the increasing influence of regional professional schools and local Beaux-Arts societies, apprenticeships continued to be the major phase in the education of western architects. These were served almost entirely in the San Francisco offices of David Farquharson, Prosper Huerne, William Mooser, and S. C. Bugbee and Son. Among Farquharson's students, the New Yorkers John J. Clark and Clinton Day eventually became partners; Prosper Huerne trained the San Francisco-born Bernhardt Henriksen; Mooser's apprentices included William Toepke and Albert Pissis—the latter, who went on to the Ecole des Beaux-Arts, enjoyed a brilliant San Francisco practice in the nineties.

In the period of the railroad the Californians continued to build houses of wood. Though Bancroft's assertion that there was not a single fine residence of brick or stone in San Francisco in 1888 is an exaggeration, nine tenths of the structures of the metropolis were frame—a higher percentage than any major city in the United States. Through the last quarter of the century the price of redwood remained constant despite a duty on foreign lumber and a brief period of inflation resulting from the southern California building boom. In addition to its availability and

[1] *California Architect and Building News*, I (Jan. 1880), 1; IV (Jan. 1883), 2, hereafter cited as *CA&BN*.

economy, redwood eminently satisfied the current demands of taste by reason of its "great facility for sawing and cutting."[2]

This last condition was significant, for if the Californians continued to use the frame construction of the previous decades, they generally eschewed the Greek Revival forms favored by the pioneers and substituted for them whatever was currently fashionable in eastern architectural circles. Contemporary photographs and sketches show that the traditional domestic style continued to be used only in the agricultural communities, and that long after urban designers succumbed to the vagaries of the Second Empire, Queen Anne, and Eastlake forms, rural builders constructed farm dwellings similar to those of the gold era. To be sure, the rural areas did not wholly escape the wonders of scalloped shingles and scroll-saw decorations. With the immigration of eastern-trained architects to the southern and valley counties, and the increased circulation of the *California Architect and Building News,* there was a return to the design uniformity so conspicuous in the fifties and sixties. By the last decades of the nineteenth century highly ornamented Queen Anne-Eastlake cottages were erected in the newly founded valley communities and in the southern California boom towns. In general, however, country architecture was conservative, and the traditional clapboard house remained the rural vernacular despite the occasional construction of a "mustard yellow" or "Indian red" bungalow in imitation of the San Francisco row house.

The academic style of the Beaux-Arts, particularly as encouraged under the building program of Napoleon III and known in the New World variously as mansard, Second Empire, and General Grant, was pre-eminently the architecture of the seventies. Properly florid and urban, the official style of the French court met the designer's need for a conscious revolt against the constraint and monotony of the earlier nineteenth-century revivals, and it satisfied the essentially parvenu nature of California's gilded age magnates, who, with few exceptions, were unre-

[2] Bancroft, *California Inter Pocula,* in *Works,* XXXV (San Francisco, 1888), 263; Sanford, *Architecture of the Southwest,* p. 247; Joseph Cather Newsom, *Picturesque and Artistic Homes and Buildings of California* (San Francisco, 1890), pp. 23-24.

lated to the Yankee and southern families making up the social enclaves of South Park and Rincon Hill.

One of the leading exponents of the new eclecticism declared that "in producing houses which suggest the Romanesque, the Eastlake, the Queen Anne and many other styles," regional architects were creating structures "peculiarly graceful and so peculiarly *Californian.*"[3] However, excepting their wooden construction, the building projects of the railroad and silver kings were similar to those of their kind everywhere in the United States in the era of the "Great Barbecue." Linden Towers, shown in Plate 45 in the full glare of the famous white paint that earned it the sobriquet "Flood's Wedding Cake," is an outstanding western example of conspicuous waste. The Flood in this case is James C., the New York-born Bonanza prince, who in 1879 commissioned Laver, Curlett and Lenzen to create an illusion of background on his San Mateo County estate. Although Linden Towers is of historical interest as the scene of an abortive attempt to unite the daughter of the house with the son of Ulysses S. Grant, its chief significance is in showing how closely California reflected the national ambitions and taste of post-Civil War America.[4]

The most celebrated setting for the "meretricious splendor" of the Second Empire was San Francisco's Nob Hill, which became fashionable about 1874 when the California Street Cable Railroad gave access to a marine view and a commanding height upon which to perch the timbered castles of a new aristocracy. These houses, described by a visiting Englishman in 1883 as having nothing to recommend them save the happy thought that they "might be swept off by a breath, and leave no trace of their existence," have, with one exception, long vanished.[5] For though a correspondent of the *California Farmer* on June 29, 1854, wishfully wrote, "Ere long we shall see our millionaires building their marble palaces of 'native marble,'" visitors in San Francisco in the seventies noted with amazement that the great houses were constructed

---

[3] Newsom, loc. cit.

[4] *CA&BN*, VIII (Feb. 1887), 20; Parsons, *California Houses*, pp. 115-117.

[5] Bishop, "San Francisco," *Harper's New Monthly Magazine*, LXVI (May 1883), 824.

almost entirely of wood. An important exception is the surviving sand-stone palace designed by Augustus Laver for James Flood on Nob Hill in 1886. But the construction of this house aroused the ill will of a considerable body of San Franciscans, who complained that the builder expended a good deal of money, which had been lost to them through silver stock speculations, on Vermont stone and eastern woods.[6]

Flood's neighbor, the railroad attorney General D. D. Colton, escaped offending the provincial tendencies of the natives, and at the same time gratified an acquired Renaissance taste, by painting the surface of his wooden house ("copied from a famous white marble palace in Italy") in imitation stonework.[7] Such a compromise was often resorted to by California's moneyed citizenry, who strove to reconcile a regional tradition, intensified by the earthquake of 1868, with a zeal for lavish display and architectural splendor. These attempts to disguise the ubiquitous redwood frame created a new color vogue in house painting and produced the famous chocolate browns, stone grays, harsh reds, and speckled yellows that wealthy builders hoped would be taken for stone.

Nothing expressed so dramatically the new age of the railroad as the great board palaces of the "Big Four" on Nob Hill. Dominating the heights of San Francisco like medieval fortresses, they were crude and pointed reminders of the railroad builder's control of the state's political and economic destiny. The worker whose job was lost to a Chinaman discharged from railroad construction, the shopkeeper whose business was ruined by the sudden flood of eastern goods, the farmer whose community was isolated when it refused subsidy to Charles Crocker—all of these found appropriate hate symbols in the architecture of Nob Hill. To San Franciscans the houses were especially repugnant. Their immense vulgarity was an ever visible affront to the older Anglo-American society of the gold era; their wooden walls were a challenge to the mobs gathered to hear Denis Kearney threaten these monstrosities with "the fate of Moscow." And yet, for all of their size and cost, the redwood castles of the railroad kings are of meager architectural significance.

[6] CA&BN, VII (May 1886), 67.
[7] Palmer, Vignettes of San Francisco, p. [10].

The single virtue of the "great gloomy barn" with bay windows on all four fronts designed for Governor Leland Stanford by Samuel Bug-bee was its supposed solidity. And this was achieved largely by contrast with the flimsy flamboyance of partner Charles Crocker's house a block or two west on California Street. The latter mansion, possibly the work of Raun and Taylor, is shown in the extreme right of Plate 53: an uncertain pile of twisted crestings, bay windows, and mansard roofs that somehow held together until earthquake and fire swept the house away. Inevitably described as a "splendid piece of renaissance building," the Crocker House is famous for a thirty-foot-high "spite fence" erected around the cottage of an offending neighbor who had refused to sell to Crocker for a reasonable price.[8] The Hopkins Mansion was the last and worst of the railroad palaces. Designed by Wright and Sanders in 1878, and likened by the editor of the *California Architect and Building News* to "a highly ornate box stove," it was compared by unknowing contemporaries to the architectural reconstructions of Viollet-le-Duc in that it brought "a bit of Carcassone to the slopes of the Pacific." The only thing substantial about the Hopkins Mansion, however, was a stone retaining wall said to have cost more to construct than the house itself; the best explanation for its construction is that Mary Hopkins wanted "to put Jane Stanford in her place."[9]

Impressive as were the Nob Hill houses in situation and cost, and determined as were their owners' wives to restrict San Francisco society to the confines of their walnut parlors, the life of the pleasure-loving city continued to be lived in the streets and public places. For if California was rapidly fitting into the national pattern of behavior, there yet remained in the seventies and early eighties—the so-called Champagne Days of San Francisco—some of the effervescence of the pioneer period. These were the days when the Bohemian haunts of Chinatown and the Italian quarter were claimed by the proper San Franciscan as his

[8] J. S. Hittell, *A Guide Book to San Francisco* (San Francisco, 1888), p. 30; Palmer, pp. [11-12].

[9] *American Architect and Building News*, XLII (Oct. 1893), 36; Scherer, *Coleman*, p. 263; Amelia (Ransome) Neville, *The Fantastic City*, ed. Virginia Brastow (Boston, 1932), p. 179; Parsons, p. 130.

own, when Norton I, "Emperor of California and Protector of Mexico," decreed his levies upon bank and bar; this was the age of the theater of Sarah Bernhardt and Mrs. John Drew, of the Poodle Dog, Marchand's, and the great hotel restaurants. Henry Adams remembered San Francisco in this period as "the most interesting city west of the Mississippi," and one with "more style than any town in the east."[10]

The Champagne Days of San Francisco were pre-eminently associated with the Palace Hotel, the architectural delight of Victorian California and long the most luxurious hostelry in America. This incredible structure, which vanished with its era in the fire of 1906, was both the supreme monument to William Ralston's ambitions and the apogee of the San Francisco style. Designed by John Gaynor, an immigrant of the sixties and architect of the neighboring Grand Hotel, the Palace was a testimony to California's self-sufficiency: the furniture, clocks, blankets, elevators, locks, and horse-hair stuffing were all of native manufacture. The immensity of the project—it covered nearly two and one-half acres and required twenty-six million bricks and forty thousand square feet of paving—is attested to in the remark of a visitor who claimed that if one wanted to hide from an enemy who lived at the Palace, the safest thing was to board there oneself.[11]

The principal design feature of Ralston's hotel was the Great Court (Plate 41), whose fragile, white vastness conveyed a sense of space and dreamlike unreality that contrasted strangely with the crowded, conventional "bird cage" exterior with its hundreds of bay windows, heavy cornice, and cemeterylike iron roof crestings (Plate 42). The Great Court, said to have been a pastiche of Viennese palace architecture, was surrounded by galleries rising seven stories to a vaulted glass roof and heated by huge braziers of polished bronze. Here some of the greatest social events in the West took place, including the reception given to General Grant upon his return to the United States in 1879, for which

[10] The Selected Letters of Henry Adams, ed. Newton Arvin (New York, 1951), p. 247.

[11] Oscar Lewis and Carroll D. Hall, Bonanza Inn: America's First Luxury Hotel (New York, 1939), pp. 19-27; San Francisco Directory, 1877, p. 23; Taylor, Between the Gates, p. 72.

occasion the court was hung with bunting and garlands and echoed to an ode sung by five hundred choristers under the direction of Madame Fabbri.

In the Baldwin Hotel, designed by John Remer for the silver speculator "Lucky" Baldwin and completed in 1877, the Palace had a single rival. But as its detractors pointed out, the Baldwin was scarcely half as large as the Palace. Nevertheless, it reflected more faithfully the grandiose and florid architecture of the Second Empire than any other structure on the coast (Plate 44). Described variously as "a monument of lavish expenditure and depraved architectural methods," and a "fabulous city in the clouds," the Baldwin was constructed of heavy timbers framed and bolted together, and it contained, in addition to a billiard parlor exclusively for women, a conservatory where the less sporting of the species could study botany. Despite the fact that a tank holding 82,000 gallons of water was built into the roof, the structure was destroyed by fire in 1898.[12]

Fortunes earned in silver, lead, and borax from Owens Valley and the Panamint Mountains were used in Los Angeles to promote such tributes to the taste of Louis Napoleon as the Baker Block and the Nadeau Hotel. The former, a mansard structure said to have cost one million dollars in 1878, is treasured in Los Angeles folklore as "the most beautiful building in the West." The Nadeau Hotel, the first four-story edifice south of Monterey, designed by Keysor and Morgan in 1882, was an architectural aberration and compares badly with the earlier Pico House, executed by the same firm to the exacting taste of the gold era. More successful southern imitations of the Palace and the Baldwin were the Tenth and Main Street Hotel, begun in Los Angeles in 1888 with a "very free treatment of the Franco-English Renaissance"; the old Arlington House at Santa Barbara, designed by Peter Barber in the Victorian bracketed style; and the Raymond Hotel in east Pasadena, whose mansard roof duplicated the style of the Louvre and whose opening in

[12] Lloyd, *Lights and Shades*, pp. 371-373; Carl Burgess Glasscock, *Lucky Baldwin* (Indianapolis, 1933), pp. 167-168; *CA&BN*, XIX (Nov. 1898), 122.

November 1886 was reported as the most brilliant event that had yet occurred in southern California.[13]

Although the mode of the Second Empire did not achieve a success in California civic architecture comparable to that won by the Romanesque, a number of mansard-type city halls were constructed in the coastal and valley cities. The most important of these was the third San Francisco City Hall (of which no photograph suitable for reproduction has been found). The subject of continuing scandal between 1871 and 1894, the city hall was originally designed by Augustus Laver, who arrived in San Francisco the year following construction of the railroad and was at the time famous in the western profession as the designer of the New York state capitol at Albany. Work had not progressed far on the San Francisco City Hall, however, before it was apparent that Laver's ambitious scheme could not be executed without greatly exceeding the one and a half million dollars allotted to the project. And when it was found that the foundations alone cost $600,000, construction was halted, the architect dismissed, and the great mansard roof eliminated from the plans.

In the period of confusion that followed, a John Clifford appeared from nowhere with a pretended gift for design and a forged letter of recommendation from the English master E. W. Pugin. Falling in with Denis Kearney, the leader of the anti-Chinese movement, Clifford became the sand-lot art critic and was so successful in assailing the reputations of San Francisco designers that he was himself appointed supervising architect of the city hall. But the hoax could not long be concealed, and Clifford was forced to resign amid a series of scandals very like those then breaking around the heads of New York's Tweed Ring. In 1888 a committee of the local chapter of the American Institute of Architects recommended that Laver's designs be carried out with only the substitution of a dome for the great tower originally planned. And,

[13] Los Angeles *Times*, May 30, 1942; Newmark, *Sixty Years*, p. 534; Glenn S. Dumke, "The Real Estate Boom of 1887 in Southern California," *Pacific Historical Review*, XI (Dec. 1942), 428; Marco R. Newmark, "Early California Resorts," *HSSCQ*, XXXV (June 1953), 144.

under the direction of Frank Shea, the whole "cyclops of a city hall, covering six and three-quarter acres," was finally completed at a cost of six
million dollars.[14]

If the provincial examples of civic building in the General Grant
style were less costly than the third San Francisco City Hall, they were
no better as architecture. Several surviving specimens are the town hall
at San Jose, designed by Theodore Lenzen in 1888, and the pattern-
book Fresno County Courthouse (Plate 43). The latter, constructed
in 1875 from plans of a local builder named A. W. Burrell, was hailed
as "the grandest and noblest edifice that has ever been planned and con-
templated in this valley." Apart from the cast-iron figures and urns, the
Fresno courthouse is closer to the Roman style of the fifties than it is to
the Second Empire. That it could have been constructed anywhere on
the California frontier where builder's pattern books were available
is proven in the erection of identical structures in Bakersfield, Modesto,
and Merced. The Fresno courthouse was enlarged in 1891-1892 in its
present Florentine-Gothic-Roman arch style by Curlett and Eisen.[15]

It was said that for an architect to be able to resist the crushing load of
banalities that the Second Empire imposed upon American taste he
would need the bravery of a pioneer and the ardor of a revolutionist.
Such qualities were abundantly possessed by Henry Hobson Richardson, who discovered in the rough stone monuments of southern France
a personal style with which to combat the falseness and vulgarity of Victorian taste. Despite the fact that Richardson's solution lay in the architecture of an age whose building requirements were wholly different
from those of the late nineteenth century, so desperate was the need for
something with which to replace the mansard terror that the Romanesque style became the civic and commercial vernacular from Massachusetts to California.

The round arch was one of the commonest architectural forms in the
United States between 1846 and 1876. In California it was used in the

[14] San Francisco Directory, 1880, pp. 16-17; CA&BN, I (Feb. 1880), 4;
IX (Oct. 1888), 127; XIV (Dec. 1893), 134-135; Out West, XVIII (Jan.
1903), 10.

[15] Lilbourne Alsip Winchell, History of Fresno County and the San Joaquin Valley (Fresno, 1933), p. 126; Bishop, p. 386; CA&BN, XII (Nov. 1891), 126.

Italian Villa style and in the important, but little known, San Francisco jail, which is presently identifiable only by a subscription list dated 1856 preserved in the Bancroft Library. It should also be noted that the eighteenth-century California missions represented the same architectural tradition that Richardson introduced into Boston church building in the early seventies. The possibilities of the crumbling Franciscan establishments as a source for an independent and regional architectural revival, however, were long ignored by Californians, who as true colonials learned their Romanesque forms from the national trade magazines, from the examples of Richardsonian railroad stations constructed throughout the West, and from the master's eastern apprentices, successors, and imitators.

One of the few California projects that can be traced to Richardson's office is the original design for the Leland Stanford Jr. University at Palo Alto, planned and partially executed between 1887 and 1891 by Richardson's successors, Shepley, Rutan and Coolidge. Richardson died before the project was broached and probably knew nothing either of Governor Stanford or the tragic fate of the young heir whose death in Italy in 1884 inspired the undertaking. The actual plan for the university was prepared by the youngest member of the firm, Charles Allerton Coolidge, from sketches and suggestions supplied by Francis A. Walker and Frederick Law Olmsted. Shepley, Rutan and Coolidge designed the Inner Quadrangle, Encina Hall, and the three small engineering buildings, which served as general classrooms. Though Mrs. Stanford insisted that the style was Moorish, the essential form and details of the first buildings at Palo Alto are Romanesque—modified to some extent by the example of the Spanish missions. The actual construction of the Outer Quadrangle and chapel was supervised by the San Francisco architectural firm of Percy and Hamilton, who designed Roble Hall and the University Museum.[16]

Despite their Richardsonian connection, Shepley, Rutan and Coolidge played a less significant role in the domestication of the Roman-

[16] Orrin Leslie Elliott, *Stanford University: The First Twenty-Five Years* (Stanford, 1937), pp. 31-32; *CA&BN*, XIV (May 1893), pls.; San Francisco *Call*, Apr. 16, 1887.

esque style on the Pacific frontier than did Richardson's Chicago imita-tors, Daniel Burnham and John Wellborn Root. If this firm's first Cali-fornia commission, the San Francisco Chronicle Building, was not a success, the office building they designed for Darius Ogden Mills in 1890 was one of the finest commercial structures in the state. After the fire of 1906, the Mills Building was extended along Bush Street to its present dimensions; in its original form, however, it adhered to the typi-cal boxlike San Francisco scheme, which resulted from a local ordinance limiting construction to a height of one hundred feet. Much of the build-ing's excellence is the result of regional atmospheric conditions permit-ting the designers to use light-colored materials, such as Inyo marble, buff-colored brick, and terra cotta. The beautiful arched entranceway was inspired by Louis Sullivan's Auditorium Building, the architectural pride of Chicago in 1890, as indeed were the grouping of windows within a series of recessed arches, the patterned brickwork, squat col-umns, and horizontal floor banding.[17]

Richardson's associate J. A. Walls, a partner in the leading Los An-geles firm of Keysor and Morgan, and the itinerant Chicago architect James M. Wood, played significant roles in popularizing the Roman-esque medium on the West Coast. Of the work of these designers, the simple, sturdy style used by Wood in his Los Angeles construction was less widely imitated than the frankly eclectic interpretations of Walls, whose first western commission was a bank for the town of Monrovia that survives as the city hall. Monrovia was a creation of the Los An-geles land rush of 1887, and it was natural that its first bank reflected the latest imported architectural style.[18]

It was perhaps the example of the Monrovia bank that led President George Sanders to remark, in his inaugural address before the San Fran-cisco Chapter of the American Institute of Architects in September 1888, that Richardson had done more to elevate the demoralized stand-ards of American architecture "than any other man of this or any age."

[17] Harriet Monroe, *John Wellborn Root* (Boston, 1896), pp. 142-143; Young, *San Francisco*, II, 754; *CA&BN*, XVI (Oct. 1895), 110; *American Architect*, L (Nov. 1895), 74.
[18] Interview with William A. Parish, Huntington Library.

Richardson's solution, Sanders concluded, restored the integrity of materials and perfected a unified style system into which every building
need could be harmoniously fitted.[19] This appeal for structural honesty
notwithstanding, one need only turn to the First National Bank Building in San Francisco, Sanders' own work, or the similar California State
Bank at Sacramento (Plate 59), to see how easily the clichés of the
style—the solid courses of rough stone, Syrian arches, and variegated
stonework—were combined in prosaic schemes showing as little feeling
for the material as they do a lack of understanding of the purpose for
which the structure was intended.[20] The practice of applying stylistic
features to a conventional metal-frame structure planned without reference to the kind of ornament that was later laid on was orthodox in nineteenth-century architectural circles, where Louis Sullivan's dictum that
form follows function was the sheerest heresy. It is ironic that Richardson's style, based upon the hope of restoring the integrity of building
materials, was so shortly converted into merely another historic mask
with which to drape an iron or steel frame.

The Romanesque Revival, irreverently likened by Willis Polk to
a "Titanic inebriation in sandstone," reached its height in the period of
the Los Angeles building boom. None of the architectural aberrations
constructed in the eighties in the "City of Diamonds" survive. But representative examples include a structure covered entirely in "pitch-
faced" ashlar and pressed brick with timbered bays and a Bavarian
watchtower, designed by Ernest Coxhead for the Young Men's Christian Association, and the Los Angeles County Courthouse, designed by
Curlett, Cuthbertson and Eisen.[21] The latter building, an unblushing
imitation of Richardson's Pittsburgh courthouse, is so clumsy a theft
that one can only conclude that the architects had not even the good
sense to make an accurate copy.

The "picturesque structures of stone and brick similar to those built
long ago in Germany and France" constructed by California viticultur-
ists among the wooded hills of Napa and Sonoma capture more success-

[19] CA&BN, IX (Oct. 1888), 128-129.
[20] CA&BN, XI (Aug. 1890), 88-89.
[21] CA&BN, IX (June 1888), 82-83; IX (Aug. 1888), 115-116.

fully the Romanesque spirit than either the office buildings of Burnham and Root or the public monuments of their numerous imitators. Indeed, the original W. B. Bourn Wine Cellar at St. Helena (Plate 56), with its arched entranceway and tower, stone mullions and transoms, low sweeping roof and well-fitted stonework, is perhaps the finest testimony to Richardson's style on the West Coast. This building and the cellar master's lodge—a two-story house constructed entirely of river-smooth boulders in the manner of the gatehouse on the Frederick Lothrop Ames Estate at North Easton, Massachusetts—were designed in 1889 by Percy and Hamilton. Other representative examples of the northern wineries, whose horizontal lines and heavy masonry walls are a striking exception to the general rural tradition of perpendicular and timbered architecture, are the buildings designed by William Mooser for the Inglenook Vineyard at Rutherford and those of the Beringer Brothers at St. Helena.[22]

Sandstone from the San Jose quarries of the pioneer architect Levi Goodrich furnished the principal building material for the northern California Romanesque productions, such as the Leland Stanford Jr. University at Palo Alto, the State Normal School at San Jose, and Bancroft's History Building at San Francisco; granite for the Los Angeles building boom was supplied by the San Bernardino stoneworks of Michael Craig. Terra cotta, popularized on the West Coast by Burnham and Root, and manufactured in the San Francisco factory of Gladding, McBean and Company and by the Los Angeles firm of W. A. Norman, was used for fire-resistant screens, as insulators for columns and beams, and for ornamental purposes. Pure white, black, gold, and blue marble taken from the base of the Inyo Mountains in Owens Valley was employed by Burnham and Root in the construction of the Mills Building; quarries at Jackson supplied the materials for the decorations of the old Academy of Sciences Building and the new San Francisco Post Office. The extensive deposits of slate above the American River, though of fine quality, were little used in the nineteenth century because of the

---

[22] Hoover, *Counties of the Coast Range*, p. 294; *CA&BN*, XIII (Oct. 1892), 114; [Lyman L. Palmer], *History of Napa and Lake Counties, California* (San Francisco, 1881), pp. 221-222.

readily available asphalt roofing materials that Californians utilized almost exclusively in commercial building from San Francisco south to the Mexican border.

Richardson's civic and commercial monuments were less crucial to the development of California architecture than his domestic work, particularly the house built for himself at Staten Island in 1868: a tall, narrow structure sheathed in clapboard and capped with a shingled mansard roof and an iron balustrade. Derived directly from the wooden cottages of the 1840's and 1850's well known in the West through the work of Andrew Jackson Downing and his regional disciple Henry William Cleaveland, the proportions and plan of Richardson's Staten Island house were duplicated by the thousands in California during the last quarter of the nineteenth century, and, in a stylistic combination of Queen Anne and Eastlake ornament, evolved into the domestic vernacular architecture known as the San Francisco style.

It is easier to describe Queen Anne architecture than to define it in terms of a historic period. The difficulty lies in the choice of a sovereign; for the style, at least as it first appeared, was closer to the building forms of the age of Queen Elizabeth I than it was to the reign of Queen Anne. In the April 1877 issue of the *American Architect* this mode is defined as "any eccentricity in general design that one can suppose would have occurred to designers one hundred and fifty or two hundred years ago."[23] As it emerged in England under the hand of Norman Shaw, the Queen Anne style was distinguished by asymmetrical planning, changing patterns of cut brick, shingles, and decorative tiles; by small-paned windows, oriels, tall chimneys, and gabled Dutch roofs. The American version of the style, articulated at Newport in 1874 in Richardson's Watts Sherman House, substituted wood for brick and tile and emphasized the picturesque rather than the historical elements of Shaw's models. In popular building circles the term Queen Anne was loosely used to cover a multitude of work that defied positive classification, and in California it was used indiscriminately with regard to the Eastlake and American Colonial forms.

Norman Shaw's early designs, with their elaborate Elizabethan and

[23] Page 134.

Flemish brick- and tilework, found accurate emulation in California only in the Alcazar Theater (Plate 47). This little-known building was erected in San Francisco in the eighties by the pioneer English architect William Patton and combines an exoticism and eclecticism unique among regional Queen Anne productions. The steeply pitched Flemish roof, for example, was hardly used in commercial construction; the tile ornaments on the second-story façade and the tiers of cut-stone bays are equally rare in California architecture. An important provincial example of the style was the Fiske Building. Constructed in Fresno in 1890 by the English-trained architect Harold Mitchell, it was considered at the time the finest commercial structure in the San Joaquin Valley. Described as "English Renaissance," the façade consisted of a series of oriels overhung by a mansard roof crowded with iron crestings and pediments carved in designs that suggest more of Eastlake than they do of Shaw.[24]

It proved impossible to introduce such genuine Queen Anne elements as brick and tile surfaces, Flemish chimneys, and slate roofs into California domestic architecture, and, characteristically, western builders merely superimposed some of the details of the style upon the traditional timbered structure whose major distinction was the ubiquitous bay window. Shortly after the *California Architect* took official notice of the Queen Anne movement in the May 1882 issue, uncertain wooden imitations of eastern models appeared in the major cities. Some examples of the style, which incidentally was attacked in the regional press as "eccentric and scrappy as a crazy quilt," include the stable in east Oakland designed by Clinton Day and featured in the October 18, 1884, number of the *American Architect;* the San Francisco residence of James V. Coleman, "in rather the select colonial order"; and the Bradbury House, erected in Los Angeles from designs of the Newsoms. The latter example, considered at the time the finest private house in southern California, incorporated all of the American Queen Anne clichés, such as a minimum of stone, a maximum of shingles, a touch of marble, "Art glass," and oak interiors.[25]

[24] *CA&BN*, XI (Apr. 1890), pl.

[25] San Francisco *Chronicle*, June 19, 1887, p. 13; J. C. Newsom, *Picturesque Homes*, No. 3 (San Francisco, 1890), Pls. [2-3].

In the spring of 1888 Curlett and Cuthbertson were commissioned by William H. Crocker to design a Queen Anne house for the site adjoining his father's Nob Hill mansion. The result is shown in Plate 53. William Curlett and Walter Cuthbertson were never long in picking up the current eastern building vogue. Crocker's house—constructed of San Francisco bluestone, pressed brick laid in red mortar, and redwood shingles and ornamented with panels in which pebbles and bits of glass were scattered in plaster after the manner of Stanford White—proved less significant as an original production than as a kind of builder's poster from which regional architects gathered details for their row houses.[26] The work of one such row-builder, William H. Lillie, is shown in Plate 60. In this project, designed for the Rountree Brothers in San Francisco, Lillie incorporated bits of brick and gravel, variegated shingles, and several bay windows and thus fulfilled Newsom's demands that "the degree of ornamentation will be governed, more or less, by the size of the builders' purse, though nowadays [1890] beauty in this form is becoming happily less and less of a luxury."[27] That not everyone was in agreement with this definition of beauty is evident in the charge made several years later by the pioneer art critic Ernest Peixotto, who condemned such houses as absurdities, "tortured with stone, brick, shingles, and slate, jumbled helter-skelter together" in a composition more Mary Anne than Queen Anne.[28]

In California the Queen Anne style was linked concurrently with the adaptation of Sir Charles Eastlake's furniture designs to create a distinctive architectural formula. The association of the two styles resulted not only from the cyclical nature of American architecture in the last decades of the century but also from the simultaneous publication of sketches of Queen Anne and Eastlake houses in the eastern architectural magazines. The Eastlake synthesis was the only international movement naturalized on the California frontier after 1869 to which regional architects made any significant contribution. For despite its popularity at the Philadelphia Centennial, and the claim of an eastern decorator that "the soothing

[26] CA&BN, X (June 1889), 79.
[27] CA&BN, XII (Mar. 1891), pls.; J. C. Newsom, Picturesque Homes, p. 24.
[28] "Architecture in San Francisco," p. 462.

influence of an Eastlake bookcase on an irritated husband has never been sufficiently calculated," the conversion of the furniture style into a vernacular architecture was largely a San Francisco phenomenon.[29]

Although the *California Architect and Building News* cursorily noted the publication of Bicknell and Comstock's collection of lithographed plates of Eastlake perspectives in November 1880, it was not until the following year that a serious attempt was made to discover the origin of the style. The editors of the *News* inquired as to whether "the monstrosities denominated 'Eastlake' " by certain San Francisco architects had anything in common with "the unique and beautiful designs projected by Charles L. Eastlake, of Leinster Square, London." The answer came from Sir Charles himself:

> I now find, to my amazement, that there exists on the other side of the Atlantic an "Eastlake style" of architecture, which, judging from the [California] specimens I have seen illustrated, may be said to burlesque such doctrines of art as I have ventured to maintain. . . . I feel greatly flattered by the popularity which my books have attained in America, but I regret that their author's name should be associated there with a phase of taste in architecture and industrial art with which I can have no real sympathy, and which by all accounts seems to be extravagant and *bizarre*.[30]

Despite this disavowal, California builders continued to erect rows of houses similar to the Eastlake Cottage (Plate 48) popularized by the San Francisco architect John C. Pelton, Jr., in a series of newspaper articles in the late seventies and reprinted in book form as *Cheap Dwellings* (San Francisco, 1882). Pelton's original model, an angular, narrow shelter sheathed in horizontal boarding and roofed with shingles, reproduced almost exactly the proportions of Richardson's Staten Island house. It was praised by the editors of the *American Architect* as "singularly well-considered, convenient, economical, and free from those strange make-shifts which mark the designs of feeble planners."[31] Much

---

[29] As quoted in Russell Lynes, *The Tastemakers* (New York, 1954), p. 105.

[30] III (Mar. 1882), 33; III (Apr. 1882), 49.

[31] John Pelton concluded that the architectural style derived directly from the de-

of the success of Pelton's designs can be attributed to the fact that, excepting for the incised ornamentation popularized in the furniture designs of Sir Charles Eastlake, they introduced no new elements into building and could easily be copied by a generation of carpenters familiar with the pattern books of Downing and Cleaveland. Their acceptance by the Real Estate Association of San Francisco, which constructed several thousand such houses at low cost under long-term financing, was also crucial in the creation of a mass row vernacular.

Within a few years of the first printing of *Cheap Dwellings*, Pelton's original model was transformed into that intricate design combination of Second Empire, Queen Anne, and Eastlake forms known as the San Francisco style (Plate 49). The emergence of what Sir Charles Eastlake called an "extravagant and *bizarre*" burlesque into an urban row vernacular resulted from the growth of mass production methods of house construction and the abundance of milling machinery available to builders in the late nineteenth century. An example of the Queen Anne–Eastlake cottage built to sell for about $1,000 is the five-room dwelling designed by Salfield and Kohlberg pictured in the *California Architect* for May 1888 and praised for its ornamented bay window and interior paneling in imitation black walnut. The two-story row houses illustrated in Plate 49 sold in San Francisco for about $3,500 and represent the final "mansard-Beaux-Arts" stage of the style. They are in the Western Addition and may have been built by the contractor-architect William F. Lewis, who constructed rows of such "lace" houses with the aid of a private millwork establishment. Similar houses could be put up by builders in Oakland for $2,500; in Los Angeles, where it was boasted that "mechanics and even day-laborers . . . have homes that delight the artist's eye," cottages of Queen Anne–Eastlake design could be purchased from $500 to $1,000. The Oriel Row (Plate 54), constructed in San Francisco in 1889 from designs of the Missouri-born architect Absalom J. Barnett, illustrates the most expensive and substantial phase of the vernacular. These houses differ from the usual row examples, however,

signs of Sir Charles Eastlake (see San Francisco *Evening Bulletin*, Nov. 12, 1881); *American Architect*, VII (Apr. 1880), 174.

only in their size and in the substitution of the London-type areaway for an exterior staircase.[32]

The economy achieved by the urban row-house builder resulted from an unvarying arrangement of floor space and a uniformity in façade planning that was scarcely belied by the millworker's art. Richardson's free use of interior space was not imitated by the California profession, and if Pelton was one of the first designers to eliminate that "old and much used or rather abused idea," the "best parlor," his floor plans were rigidly formal with hall areas designed only for circulation. Invariably the façade of the San Francisco row house was sharply divided into two perpendicular sections, one consisting of a porch supported by champagne-glass columns, and the other occupied by the bay windows (Plate 49). Though the heavily decorated exterior surface reflected the limitless possibilities that milled ornamentation presented to the builder, there was no attempt to falsify the wooden construction, and for all of their crests and scrolls and brackets the urban row dwellings have an appearance of airy lightness. Pelton and his colleagues rebelled against "leaden hues draped in sable fringes" and painted their houses green, yellow, peach, sage, Indian red, and vermilion. While fashionable decorators stressed the importance of oak, redwood was used almost entirely in the exterior and interior construction. The woodwork for mantels, screens, staircases, wainscoting, and doors was factory made and cheaply purchased. Interior plastic surfaces, known as "scratch," had considerable vogue and were usually tinted in gold, bronze, or moss green. Art glass was recommended as "an aid to the architect in his persistent efforts for beautiful effects."[33]

The distinguishing feature of the California row house was neither its ingenious combination of architectural styles nor its relative cheapness —it was the bay window. For these billowing sheets of glass were to San Francisco of the seventies and eighties what the brownstone front was to New York of the same period. Like the cocktail, the bay window has been claimed as a regional invention. Pelton, whose houses were never

[32] CA&BN, X (Sept. 1889), souvenir ed., unnumbered pp.; Walter Lindley and J. P. Widney, California of the South (New York, 1888), p. 92.

[33] Pelton, p. 43; CA&BN, III (May 1882), 67; J. C. Newsom, Picturesque Homes, pp. 25-26.

without a bay, claimed its origin in "our fanciful bird-cage imagina-tions"; the English traveler Ben Taylor, writing in 1878, insisted that California architecture should be called the "bay-window order," and he accurately ascribed the secret of these "stately fronts . . . with all the windows gracefully leaping out of themselves" as testimony to San Francisco's insistence upon maximum light.[34] Between 1867 and 1885 not less than 95 per cent of all dwellings in San Francisco had one or more bays. Indeed, these windows were so much a part of the city's ar-chitecture that special building regulations were framed to govern their height and projection in relation to the public sidewalks. Appearing first as timid bulges in the frame buildings of gold-rush San Francisco, the bay window remained uncommon until the authority of the New England house with its piazza was challenged by the mansard–Queen Anne–Eastlake conglomerate style. The veranda, though admirably adapted to a warm climate, was not suited to San Francisco, where fog and close ur-ban planning placed a premium on sunlight. The early bays of the sixties, simple rectangular projections, gradually swelled out into vast prows of glass to reach their apogee in the Palace Hotel, which had almost seven hundred such protuberances (Plate 42). Because the bay window ad-mirably met the demands of light, convenience, space, and sanitation, every architectural style domesticated on the West Coast was altered to accommodate it.

Under such headings as "A Carpenter's Frenzy" and "Saw and Hatchet Artistry," the San Francisco row vernacular was castigated in the press as a "discouraging procession of wooden, bay-windowed, snub-roofed, shoulder-to-shoulder structures . . . browbeaten by the old fear of the *temblor*"; its ornamented façade was scornfully likened to the "puffing, paint and powder of our female friends" and to a jumble of "bird cages, vegetable crates, dog kennels, sewing baskets, [and] wed-ding cakes."[35] The regional critic Ernest Peixotto condemned the move-ment as a mask for "a multitude of sins" in which "every tenet of architec-

[34] Pelton, p. 50; Taylor, *Between the Gates*, pp. 72-73.

[35] *Out West*, XVIII (Jan. 1903), 4; *CA&BN*, IX (Oct. 1888), 129; *Archi-tect and Engineer*, II (Oct. 1905), 87; Newton J. Tharp, "What Bad There Is and What Good There Might Be in Inexpensive Architecture," *Overland Monthly*, 2nd Ser., XXXVI (Dec. 1900), 532-538.

ture has been violated," and Harold Mitchell, who himself was responsible for some fairly representative examples, recommended that designers in this medium be "skewered with antique pins upon one of their
'so-called' Eastlake elevations."[36] And yet no matter to what extent the
ideas of Norman Shaw and Sir Charles Eastlake were altered to create
the jaunty lines of the comfortable little houses with their pierced and
painted fronts and jutting bay windows, the speculative row houses of the
California cities provided efficiently planned, well-lighted, and sanitary
shelter to the large number of lower- and middle-income families usually
ignored by the architect. It was a style, moreover, equally suited to the
rich and the poor and had the necessary advantage of not demanding
too much skill on the part of the architect or builder.

Though the Queen Anne–Eastlake medium was primarily an inexpensive urban vernacular, it was much favored by builders of country
houses and resort hotels. In fact the style seemed especially congenial to
the latter's needs, and its adaptability to outdoor sleeping areas, glass
porches, loggias, and open sitting rooms is demonstrated in the great
timbered, towered, and glazed railroad caravansaries at Coronado and
Del Monte. The Hotel Del Coronado, completed in 1888, was the
work of the newly arrived Reid brothers. The enormously admired
Hotel Del Monte, probably the largest Eastlake conception of the century, inspired an English traveler to remark that if California architects
did not always follow eastern styles, "when they really attempt something
in the same line, they are likely as not to do it a great deal better."[37]

As was noted earlier in this chapter, through the whole of the last
century the California farmhouse embodied the colonial tradition of a
plain, clapboard, frame structure with a piazza along the front or at the
side. In the smaller towns, such as San Diego, Santa Rosa, and San Jose,
however, the reigning urban architectural style was jealously aped. Thus
an English visitor to the latter community in the mid-eighties wrote, "as
in most other provincial towns," its buildings are "covered with bay-
windows, in what might be described as the San Francisco style of archi-

[36] Peixotto, p. 461; CA&BN, III (Feb. 1882), 29; VI (Nov. 1885), 182-
183.
[37] Bishop, p. 370.

tecture."[38] The Banta House at Pasadena, constructed by the carpenter-architect Eugene Getschell in 1886, is a surviving example of the transplanted urban dwelling (Plate 52).[39] Getschell's design is representative in its use of scalloped shingles, shifting wood patterns, and squares of colored glass; less typical is its treatment of the mansard-roofed tower in which the usual bays have been replaced by a two-story porch decorated with turned and incised ornaments. The several picture books published by the Newsoms between 1885 and 1890 are another source for rural specimens of the San Francisco row house, selected in every case, according to the authors, to demonstrate that "in the matter of *Picturesque and Comfortable Homes* we [Californians] may justly lay claim to the palm."[40]

The cycle of revivals that congealed in the decade and a half after 1869 into the Second Empire–Queen Anne–Eastlake combination reached its climax in the Carson House, designed by Samuel and Joseph Newsom for a lumber magnate in Eureka in 1885 (Plates 50 and 51).[41] A photograph of this house is included along with the architects' drawing to demonstrate that though the original conception might seem to defy the limits of practical carpentry, every detail was faithfully executed in all-too-pliable redwood. A comparison of the Carson House with the San Francisco row illustrated in Plate 49 reveals that the Newsoms did not introduce any new elements into their Eureka design; in each case the fenestration represents a common French origin, the variegated-wood treatment is similar, and both city and town examples are equally tortured with crests, brackets, scrolls, and finials. The uniqueness of the Carson House, relative to the Bay Area "lace" vernacular from which it is derived, is simply that there is so much of it. For this structure is not only a tribute to the exuberance and self-confidence of the Victorians, but also a testimony to the artistic confusion that accompa-

[38] Ibid., p. 349.

[39] Interview with William A. Parish, Huntington Library.

[40] J. C. Newsom, *Picturesque Homes*, p. 23.

[41] Samuel and Joseph Newsom, *Picturesque California Homes*, No. 2 (San Francisco, n.d.), pls.; Federal Writers' Project, *California: A Guide to the Golden State* (New York, 1939), p. 354; Sanford, p. 247.

nied the cycle of architectural revivals on the West Coast. For with the exception of the Romanesque, every one of the eastern styles domesti-cated on the California frontier between the Gothic and Colonial Re-vivals is contained within this single design.

Of late the Carson House has been discovered by an increasing num-ber of Neo-Victorians, who find in its spacious rooms, mahogany-paneled nooks, and great halls an escape from the cramped, unimagi-native, and bleak dimensions of contemporary housing. Its historical importance, however, is as a supreme architectural example of the ten-sions and conflicts in California post-Civil War society. It is the best sur-viving example of what happened in architecture when California was swept into the main stream of national ambition and taste. The great promise of pioneer architecture, nourished by two decades of economic and cultural isolation, was submerged in a cycle of eastern revivals. But if the Carson House embodies the worst features of the Victorians, such as its sham substantiality and artistic confusion, it remains both wondrous and exotic—a monument to a restless and troubled age that refused to countenance a plain surface, a continuous line, or a uniform material. After the Carson House there was nowhere to go but back into the colonial past.

VI. THE DISCOVERY OF THE PAST

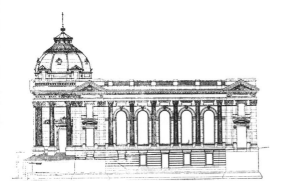

In the last decade of the nineteenth century California uncovered its
architectural past. The discovery was characteristically colonial, for
the mission movement developed out of an eastern revival domesticated
on the California frontier by immigrant architects. This was the American Colonial Revival, whose genesis, the New England exhibit at the
Philadelphia Centennial of 1876, created the desire for beamed ceilings, small-paned windows, and high mantels that led Stanford White
to revive a native architecture. But though Californians cried that they,
too, wanted "to live amid wainscoting, nestle in elliptical arched nooks
. . . and go up to bed over boxed stairs with ramped rails and twisted bal-
usters," the interest in early American architecture on the Pacific Coast
was brief.[1] For the Californians were uncertainly discovering that they
had a past of their own. As one of them put it, "Give me neither Romanesque nor Gothic; much less Italian Renaissance, and least of all English
Colonial—this is California—give me Mission."[2] The transformation
of the Colonial Revival into a native mission movement at the end of the
nineteenth century signified the disappearance of the architectural frontier and the emergence of California regionalism.

[1] As quoted in Vincent J. Scully, *The Shingle Style* (New Haven, 1955), p. 45.
[2] As quoted in Felix Rey, "A Tribute to Mission Style," *Architect and Engineer*,
LXXIX (Oct. 1924), 78.

It was not until six years after the Philadelphia Centennial that the editors of the *California Architect and Building News* took official note of the Colonial Revival by publishing the winning designs in a national competition for an inexpensive country house sponsored by the San Francisco Chapter of the American Institute of Architects.[3] These designs, all by eastern architects in the new "colonialized" version of the Queen Anne style, served the Californians as models for participation in yet another imported revival. The house designed by William Mooser for Captain Thomas Mein in Oakland and illustrated in Plate 63 is typical of the imitative work inspired by this competition. Mooser, a Swiss immigrant of the fifties, presumably knew nothing of American Colonial architecture other than what he had seen reproduced in builders' trade journals, and certainly there is little of the colonial spirit in this incongruous design with bay windows joined to a façade scheme including an outsized Federal porch, Adams' windows, and classic pilasters. A single surviving example of institutional work in this medium is the former Lick Wilmerding School in San Francisco by Curlett and McCaw—an extremely simple two-story frame structure with dormer windows that demonstrates the return, after almost half a century, to the clapboard and shingle architecture of the gold rush.[4]

But the Colonial Revival had little in common with the famous style introduced on California's architectural frontier by Thomas Larkin and Walter Colton. And despite the tradition of the Yankee frame house from the colonial period to the coming of the railroad, the revival of early American architecture in California as articulated by the eastern firm of McKim, Mead and White was brief. Charles Augustus Keeler spoke for the profession when he wrote that if in the eastern states the colonial houses had an appropriateness and charm resulting from the natural use of good materials and the basic simplicity of colonial building requirements, their "meaningless white-painted fluted columns of hollow wood" and "little balconies of turned posts" were wholly incongruous when set down amid the glare, newness, and rush of western

[3] *CA&BN*, V (Aug. 1884), 140-145; V (Sept. 1884), 157-162.
[4] *CA&BN*, XVIII (Dec. 1897), pls.; XX (June 1899), pls.

life.[5] Better the robust extravagance of the San Francisco Queen Anne–Eastlake row houses, cried the critics, than the sequestering of any more "Puritan" dwellings of the type deservedly lampooned by John Wellborn Root as "so white and bloodless as to be strongly suggestive of a prolonged cold-water diet."[6]

The most interesting development in the Colonial Revival was the phase sometimes called the shingle style, which reached the coast through the immigration of Willis Polk, the *enfant terrible* of western architecture of the late nineteenth century. Son of a southern architect whose practice ended with the Civil War, Polk admitted to being the leading designer in the Southwest before he was twenty years old. Arriving in San Francisco in 1886, "just about the time that architecture struck the town," as he expressed it, Polk launched the first number of the *Architectural News* in November 1890. Though his magazine went through only three issues before Polk skipped to Carmel with the subscription money, it prepared the way for the Mission Revival and set the tone for sophisticated building in California for a quarter of a century.

In the work of Willis Polk the various phases of the Colonial Revival in California found their fullest expression. Plate 57, a sketch for a projected house in San Francisco from the second number of the *Architectural News*, shows the transition stage from Queen Anne to Colonial by the application of picturesque chimneys, leaded casements, and changing brick and wood patterns to a perfectly symmetrical eighteenth-century façade. The houses he designed in Los Angeles and Santa Monica in collaboration with Ernest Coxhead (illustrated in Polk's drawings in the *American Architect* of July 1888) combine Flemish gables and Tudor trappings with a captain's walk and colonial clapboarding. In the house planned several years later by Polk and A. Page Brown for the Towne family in San Francisco, the classic details emerge austere and authentic, with almost no concession to the picturesque elements so beloved by row-house builders in the eighties. Finally, in the much altered Avery House in Sausalito—a horizontal box in split cedar shingles finished in

[5] *The Simple Home* (San Francisco, 1904), pp. 23-24.
[6] As quoted in Monroe, *Root*, p. 187.

waxed redwood paneling—Polk returned to the simplicity of Richardson's Atlantic Coast cottages.[7]

If McKim, Mead and White's Colonial Revival was indifferently received in California, their neoclassic public style reigned unchallenged on the Pacific Coast for a half century. The neoclassic movement, like the earlier Colonial Revival, was launched by an international exposition—this time the World's Columbian at Chicago in 1893. The immense success of the "Academic Reaction" on California's architectural frontier resulted less from the fame of the "White City" at Chicago, however, than from the failure of the regional Beaux-Arts groups to produce anything significant despite a monopoly of the state's architectural offices and journal. A typical example of the Beaux-Arts answer to the iron buildings of the seventies and the Romanesque piles of the eighties is Salfield and Kohlberg's Rosenthal Building (Plate 55), whose single virtue is in displaying in one scheme every cliché that the academically trained architect was capable of reproducing. Both David Salfield and Hermann Kohlberg arrived in California in the eighties, the latter with some years service as a government architect and a too accurate memory of the Teutonic Beaux-Arts villas of Frankfort and Stuttgart. Fortunately, the German interpreted Beaux-Arts period was brief, and the plan of the same architects for a San Joaquin County courthouse in the tradition of the Rosenthal Building was never carried out.[8]

After the Rosenthal Building, it is refreshing to consider the extant Bradbury Building in Los Angeles, the most significant commercial design from the decade of the nineties and one of the few buildings not influenced by the neoclassic reaction. The circumstances regarding this structure are as unusual as the finished project. The architect, George Herbert Wyman, came to California for his health in 1891. Without formal training in design or construction, he took a brief apprenticeship in the office of an uncle and later worked as a draftsman for Sumner P. Hunt, who received a commission from Louis Bradbury for a commercial building on Broadway at Third Street. For some reason the work

[7] *American Architect*, XXXV (Feb. 6, 1892), pl.
[8] *CA&BN*, VII (Dec. 1886), 175, 177; X (Sept. 1889), pl.

was taken from Hunt and offered to Wyman, who accepted the challenge after communing with his dead brother over a planchette. The result was a masterpiece.

The Bradbury Building, completed in 1893, was inspired by the architect's infatuation with the California light and by a description of a utopian building in Edward Bellamy's *Looking Backward*. This fictional structure was "a vast hall full of light, received not alone from the windows on all sides but from the dome, the point of which was a hundred feet above. . . . The walls were frescoed in mellow tints, to soften without absorbing the light which flooded the interior."[9]

This quotation will serve as sufficient description of the interior of the Bradbury Building itself and compensates for the wholly inadequate impression conveyed by photographs. Because the site offered Wyman no possibilities other than those that were usual in urban commercial planning, he contented himself with an exterior of chaste Sullivanesque proportions in brown brick, sandstone, and terra cotta, and concentrated all of his talents upon the great court—the "vast hall full of light." Here he created a remarkable effect of hazy sunlight by using walls of glazed brick in rose and gold, pale yellow floor tiling, stair treads and sills of rich brown marble, and gold-grained woodwork. Light enters from the glass roof as well as from a band of clerestory windows, below which runs a frieze of brown terra cotta. In contrast to this "sunset glow," Wyman left exposed and painted black all structural iron parts in the court, such as galleries, staircases, and elevator shafts. The Bradbury Building was Wyman's single important work and was ignored in contemporary architectural circles. The Californians, as usual, were looking to the East and sought salvation in yet another imported revival.

Even before the "White City" took form in Chicago in 1893, a small band of San Franciscans determined that only a return to the classic sources could save architecture from the perverted inanities of the German Beaux-Arts movement. Their slogan was "refinement and restraint as well as zest," and their leader, the ebullient Willis Polk, was en-

[9] As quoted in Esther McCoy, " 'A Vast Hall Full of Light': The Bradbury Building, 1893," *Arts and Architecture*, LXX (Apr. 1953), 21.

shrined as the inaugurator of what is now regarded as a regional renais-sance.[10] Certainly Polk and A. Page Brown did their best through the pages of the *Architectural News* and through their coterie of high-living enthusiasts to start a number of young men upon "the civilized adven-ture." The earliest results of this movement were the second Hibernia Bank and the Crocker Building, both constructed in San Francisco in 1891.

The Hibernia Bank, still standing on the northwest corner of McAl-lister and Jones streets, is the work of the Beaux-Arts-trained Albert Pissis in collaboration with William Moore. Pissis' beautifully rendered drawing, certainly a consideration in winning its architects the Hibernia commission, is reproduced in Plate 58. The design, as finally executed, is surprisingly pure and, excepting for an overworked copper dome, ex-hibits a rare independence from the usual clichés of the Ecole. Willis Polk at once named the bank the most beautiful building in California, despite its selection as such by a score of local architects—"twenty bumps of presumption," the young rebel termed them—and he praised Pissis especially for violating the current architectural code by disdaining to employ in a single commission every known building material and style.[11]

It is thought that Willis Polk shares some responsibility with A. Page Brown for the old Crocker Building, completed shortly after the Hiber-nia Bank on an awkward pie-shaped lot at the intersection of Market and Post streets. Of obvious Roman derivation, the Crocker Building rises in a series of heavily rusticated arches from monolithic Ionic columns and is faced discordantly in yellow and brown brick. The building was criti-cized in the *American Architect* for its apparent absence of strength re-sulting from the continuation of the structure some three stories above the cornice.[12] Brown's contemporary Ferry Building is a better example of the architect's talent in combining classic forms and details. It is again

---

[10] Frederick Hamilton, "The World of Willis Polk & Company," *Architect and Engineer*, XXIV (Apr. 1911), 35.

[11] *CA&BN*, X (Oct. 1889), 132; Polk as quoted in *The Wave*, IX (1892), 8.

[12] *CA&BN*, XIV (Mar. 1893), pl.; *American Architect*, XXXV (Jan. 1892), 11-12. See also Peixotto, pp. 454-455.

strikingly Roman in feeling and bears a rather close resemblance to Shepley, Rutan and Coolidge's South Station in Boston. Unfortunately, the splendid peristyle designed by Polk for this monument was never executed; the drawing is preserved in the Department of Architecture of the University of California at Berkeley.

With all their revolutionist airs, California's neoclassic designers demonstrated as little regard for the unity of form and function as their Victorian teachers. When Pissis built the present Emporium Building in San Francisco in 1895, he felt compelled to conceal its steel scaffold behind a solid masonry façade in imitation of a Roman arch; contemporary Los Angeles architects followed his lead with such buildings as the Wilcox Block and the Hotel Van Nuys, whose modern construction is masked by stone fronts bearing a succession of architectural orders.[13] Though the problem of the soaring skyscraper wrapped in antique dress was not serious in San Francisco, where very tall buildings were limited by ordinance to Market Street, such structures as qualified for this class were handled with the same lack of imagination that marked the work of less adroit designers of the seventies. The single example to survive the fire of 1906 is the Claus Spreckels Building, designed by the Reid brothers at the end of the century; however, its great Roman arch, which bore sixteen stories of superimposed ornament into a cloud of domes, cupolas, and lanterns, disappeared in recent reconstructions.[14]

The "Academic Reaction" had little effect upon California domestic architecture, although there were a few imitations of the high-renaissance style of McKim, Mead and White. The house Ernest Coxhead constructed in 1893 for George Whittell was done in the manner of the Cancelleria Palace, and even the much-grumbling critic Ernest Peixotto admitted it would be "one of the chief architectural attractions among San Francisco residences."[15] Some extant examples from this period are the W. B. Bourn and Wohler houses, both constructed in San Francisco in 1896. The former, illustrated in Plate 62, is a fine specimen

[13] *CA&BN*, XV (July 1894), pls.

[14] *American Architect*, LVII (Aug. 28, 1897), pls.

[15] Peixotto, p. 462. The designer's drawing is reproduced in *CA&BN*, XV (Apr. 1894), 40.

of the austere Georgian-Italian style so much favored by Willis Polk. The Wohler House, by the Spanish-trained J. E. Molera, suffers from the limitations of its wood construction and from the architect's excessive use of detail.[16] A more interesting structure is Bourn's stone cottage in Grass Valley. Designed by Willis Polk with walls of roughhewn granite trimmed with brick, it was described in the San Francisco *Chronicle* of May 2, 1897, as "without parallel in California." These houses, however, had little influence upon contemporary designers, who already were engrossed in the mission experiment.

In February 1882 a group of Californians, reacting against a century of European and northeastern American architectural colonialism, launched a revolution that culminated a decade later in the Mission Revival. The prominent San Francisco designer Harold Mitchell began the attack with an appeal for a genuinely native architecture shaped by "its fitness for the purpose for which it is to be erected" and "the locality where it is to stand." How rarely contemporary building met this standard is evident in the question raised two months later by Theodore Eisen. In an address before the San Francisco Chapter of the American Institute of Architects he asked whether the "primitive huts" of the "barbarous ages" were not more consistent with the wants and customs of their times than the California "models of classic architecture, with Frisco-American variations" that concealed an honest wood construction beneath a façade of imitation masonry and scroll-sawed decorations. This query by San Jose's leading architect had already been anticipated in an article in the *Overland Monthly*, in which a critic charged, "There is not upon the face of the civilized earth . . . a large city whose buildings are, as a whole, so utterly devoid of all architectural merit as are those of San Francisco."[17]

Although many of the attacks upon western architectural standards that followed the remarks of Mitchell and Eisen reflected the personal jealousies and intense competition characteristic of the depressed profes-

[16] *American Architect*, LIII (Aug. 8, 1896), pls.; *CA&BN*, XVII (Mar. 1896), pls.

[17] *CA&BN*, III (Feb. 1882), 29; III (Apr. 1882), 53; *Overland Monthly*, 1st Ser., XV (Sept. 1875), 283.

sion in the eighties and nineties, the real issue—independence from a century of colonial leading strings—was never forgotten. "We have seen a Gothic revival, a Queen Anne craze, a Romanesque period," cried one embattled architect, "and now because it is the fashion to study architecture in Paris, we must submit for the time being to the constant assertion of modern French Renaissance."[18]

In the first number of the *Architectural Record* it was claimed that California required a different kind of architecture from that of the Atlantic seaboard from which the successive revivals had come—a style rooted in regional conditions and needs. Two years earlier, in December 1889, the editor of the *California Architect and Building News* suggested that in the "Mission or Morisco" mediums lay the solution to the problem of a native architecture. But the awakening of the Californians to the architectural possibilities of their colonial past was a slow and uncertain arousal. For though San Franciscans celebrated the centennial of the founding of Mission Dolores the same year that they discovered the New England exhibit at Philadelphia, the Mission Revival was ten years getting under way. The gradual evolution of the Queen Anne style toward a native colonial architecture, which so facilitated the Early American Revival in the East, had no western counterpart, and the California revivalists were faced with the fact that, excepting some poor adobe cottages, the only architectural remains from their colonial past were the isolated ruins of the Franciscan missions (Plate I).

Charles Fletcher Lummis, chauvinistic editor of *Land of Sunshine*, is generally credited with launching the Mission Revival. And in a purely literary sense this is true. Among the first to realize the cultural and financial opportunities of the long-neglected California missions, Lummis spoke for the real estate promoters when he wrote that the missions "are worth more money, are a greater asset to Southern California, than our oil, our oranges, or even our climate," and " a man is a poor fool who thinks he can do business without sentiment."[19] The latter quality was

[18] *A History of the New California*, ed. Leigh Hadley Irvine (New York, 1905), I, 320.

[19] As quoted in Franklin Dickerson Walker, *A Literary History of Southern California* (Berkeley, 1950), p. 132.

abundantly supplied by Lummis, who, with the aid of the prominent southern California architects Sumner Hunt and Arthur Benton, wrote a series of articles in the mid-nineties on the suitability of Spanish Colonial building traditions as a basis for a native California architecture.

The first architect to become seriously aware of the possibilities that the missions offered contemporary builders was Willis Polk, who devoted part of each issue of the *Architectural News* to articles on the Franciscan establishments, which he illustrated with drawings of mission details. It is uncertain at what date Polk realized the architectural potentialities of the missions, but as early as 1887 he made a sketch for an imaginary "Mission Church of Southern California Type," and it is claimed that the architect's greatest pride was his role in rehabilitating Mission Dolores, in the course of which he studied Spanish tilemaking and Franciscan methods of construction.[20]

It was another easterner, Polk's friend and collaborator A. Page Brown, who brought the movement to national attention with his design for the California Building at the Columbian Exposition in Chicago. This design, selected in a competition limited to entries in the so-called Mission-Moorish medium, was a patchwork of stylized Franciscan forms to be executed in a mixture of rough cement that successfully imitated adobe.[21] A correspondent to the *American Architect* pointed out that the winning project was only vaguely mission, and that it had as many Japanese and Beaux-Arts elements as Franciscan. A better design, he added, was one submitted by Bernard Maybeck, which was "unmistakably Californian" and conjured up "sweet memories of blue skies, eternal sunshine, the dark olive green of nature, woods and gold balls of fruit."[22] Considering the quality of Maybeck's surviving work, such as the Palace of Fine Arts in San Francisco and the First Church of Christ, Scientist, in Berkeley, it is regrettable that his design was neither executed nor preserved. With all its failings, however, Brown's scheme was judged by Montgomery Schuyler "an admirable piece of picturesque

[20] *Architectural News,* I (Nov., Dec. 1890), passim.
[21] *Architectural Record,* III (July-Sept. 1893), 61-62.
[22] XXXV (Mar. 1892), 187.

architecture, and one of the noteworthy ornaments of the Fair."[23] And with its red tile roof, long arcades, and classical details, the California Building compares favorably with what Louis Sullivan called the "drooling imbecility" of the majority of the state buildings.

In his design for the Manufactures and Liberal Arts Building at the California Midwinter Fair held in San Francisco in 1894, Brown stressed authenticity rather than fantasy—or at least authenticity in detail. The materials used in the construction of the Manufactures and Liberal Arts Building were similar to those experimented with at Chicago, although on this occasion Brown tinted his walls in light colors "after the manner of the Orient."[24] The artistic, and financial, success of the World's Columbian Exposition led the organizing committee of the Midwinter Fair to consider employing only those eastern firms responsible for the "White City" at Chicago, and Brown was to be the single California representative on the board of architects. The committee reckoned, however, without the regional profession, whose position was that "if there is carrion in this, why not let the local vultures have their share."[25] Among those added to the committee were E. R. Swain and Samuel Newsom; the appointment of the latter was especially unfortunate, for his Agricultural and Horticultural Hall—whether Moorish, Indian, or Franciscan—demonstrated on an immense scale how easily the mission style could become ridiculous.

The conditions that gave distinction and charm to the Spanish missions—their open situation and simplicity of need—were not factors in late nineteenth-century urban building requirements. It is hardly remarkable, therefore, that when the style was applied to contemporary structures the results were uniformly disastrous. In church construction (the only area where the mission example could be expected to find successful imitation), the Gothic tradition was too strong to be challenged; the so-called mission railroad stations constructed by the Southern Pa-

[23] *Architectural Record*, III (July-Sept. 1893), 61.

[24] *California Midwinter International Exposition 1894* (San Francisco, 1894), passim.

[25] *American Architect*, XLII (Nov. 1893), 59.

cific were patterned after Richardson's Massachusetts models and cannot qualify as Franciscan adaptations. The same can be said for the first buildings at Stanford University, praised at the time by eastern critics as the finest embodiment of the California Colonial style. For if the Palo Alto buildings suggest, especially in their planning, elements common to both the Romanesque and mission styles, they are properly part of the Romanesque Revival that reached California a decade before the mission style was discovered.

Excepting A. C. Schweinfurt's Examiner Building (Plate 64) constructed in San Francisco in 1898 of rough plaster over brick and decorated with Franciscan designs in terra cotta and Numidian marble, the Mission Revival failed to produce a single office building of distinction.[26] The commercial projects of the famous mission protagonist A. Page Brown illustrate the problems that a sensitive designer faced in attempting to adapt a primitive architecture to an industrial society. In only one case, the Builders' Exchange constructed in 1895 in San Francisco, was Brown able to convey at least a suggestion of the stark, elongated character of the California missions. This was achieved by an extreme simplicity in ornament and the use of a horizontal scheme—a solution rarely possible in townsite planning. More typical of his work are the Sainte Claire Clubhouse in San Jose and the Atkinson Building in San Francisco, in which Spanish-baroque, Tuscan Villa, and Venetian forms are chaotically blended in design patterns that defy identification.[27] Brown's colleague J. S. Cahill resorted to the usual shifts of the Mission Revivalists in his prize-winning design for the Native Sons of the Golden West by reducing the characteristic arcade to a narrow window embrasure and pitching the roof so steeply that only cast-iron tiles could be used. Typically, the so-called mission details of this building were borrowed from Romanesque models used in commercial construction for a decade.

Efforts to fit Franciscan architectural forms to house construction were hardly more successful. For as a mission apologist admitted in Charles Fletcher Lummis' vigorously partisan *Land of Sunshine*, "The style is not easily adapted to modern uses, and requires a master designer

[26] Ibid., LIX (Feb. 19, 1898), pls.
[27] *CA&BN*, XVI (Dec. 1895), pl.

to preserve breadth and proportion without sacrificing sunlight, ventila-
tion and convenience."[28] In only half a dozen cases was this achieved,
notably in the Golden Gate Park Lodge in San Francisco and the Tevis
House in Bakersfield, where secluded sites and large budgets permitted
the architect to recapture some of the charm of the original Franciscan
buildings.[29] The Park Lodge, designed by Edward R. Swain in 1896
and illustrated in Plate 61, is the best extant Mission Revival house in
California. It has not only an unusual site advantage, but its wide, useful
arcades and deeply overhanging tile roof have structural as well as aesthetic importance. Further, the stone building materials used by Swain
give a sense of solidity altogether lacking in traditional mastic or stucco
Mission Revival construction.

The typical mission bungalow was patterned after the design of John
Knapp, who at the end of the century attempted to create a mass domestic
vernacular in the mission style. The original model, featured in the *California Architect and Building News* for May 1899, was constructed of
whitewashed stucco and was advertised to sell for $1,500. Although
the emphasis on economy gave the cottage a simplicity that might pass
for authenticity, its chief characteristic is the sacrifice of substance for
sham. How many of Knapp's sterile little bungalows, with their band of
imitation tiles and meager plaster-and-lath arches, were constructed in the
colonies for which they were planned is not known, but his model—
furnished with Bagdad cloth and arts-and-craft furniture—may well be
the genesis of the stucco bungalow that was so much a part of American
architecture in the first quarter of the twentieth century.

Despite the statement of Rexford Newcomb that California, "true
daughter of Old Spain," had "forsaken pretty largely the Anglo-Saxon
forms of her American population in favor of . . . her Hispanic past," the
Mission Revival failed because it proved impossible to adapt the primitive architecture of a religious order to the commercial and worldly society of the late nineteenth century.[30] No one, of course, suggested that
the architect construct his mission office building or bungalow in the

[28] *Land of Sunshine*, IV (Feb. 1896), 130.
[29] *CA&BN*, XVI (Apr. 1895), pl.; XVII (June 1896), pls.
[30] Newcomb, *Old Mission Churches*, p. 358.

mud-block tradition of the adobe builders. As Charles Keeler early pointed out, the attempt to fit an ecclesiastical and medieval architecture to modern life must result in the debasement of form and the falsification of materials. And just as the designers of Tuscan villas and Queen Anne houses recast their imported models in redwood, so the Mission Revivalists constructed their projects with hollow arches and imitation tiles. Given this fact, it is difficult to understand how the influential *Craftsman* could praise the style for meeting its criterion "to employ only those forms and materials which make for simplicity, individuality and dignity of effect."[31] Apparently the editors of the *Craftsman* formed their conception of the Mission Revival from the Franciscan originals and failed to distinguish these from the lath-and-plaster imitations.

With the failure of the mission movement the regional mythmakers launched the Spanish Revival, the final development in California's search for a romantic past. Though not a part of the state's architectural frontier, the new style was actually what Lummis and his friends were attempting to promote. In fact, if there had been any adequate secular Spanish Colonial building, the unsuccessful attempt to derive a commercial and residential vernacular architecture from the example of the missions would not have been necessary. Thus, when the mission movement proved inadequate, the Spanish Revivalists set about creating a past even more legendary than that manufactured by the mission propagandists.

One of the first to explore the possibilities of a Spanish Revival was Herbert Croly, who urged Californians to go back to the original—the Mediterranean houses—which he claimed the Franciscan friars misrepresented because of their ignorance of the art of building and the lack of proper materials, tools, and craftsmen. These buildings, wrote Croly, constitute the most "valuable and imitable local domestic style."[32] But, as an investigation of the work of the adobe builders in Chapter I made manifest, there were no "Mediterranean" houses in California to return to. And unlike the genuine colonial world that eastern architects drew upon for inspiration in the American Colonial Revival, the Spanish Colonial culture of California had to be manufactured.

[31] I (Oct. 1901), foreword; II (Feb. 1902), 36-37.
[32] "The California Country House," *Architect and Engineer*, VII (Dec. 1906), 25.

In 1896 an alliance was formed between the Southern California Chapter of the American Institute of Architects and the Pasadena Loan Association "for the purpose of collecting and maintaining public exhibitions of all that is best in architectural design . . . of that noble art to whose triumphs the older Spain and Italy owe so much of their charm." The examples selected, however, tended to be more Algerian than Alhambran, and for each Venetian palace there were as many Arabian mosques. Indeed, the results of this premature revival, more amusing than serious, included a design for an Alameda residence with Indian turrets and Islamic decorations, a Granada Court in plaster for the Gail Borden estate in the San Gabriel Valley, and the aquamarine- and amethyst-glass domes of the Theosophical Temple and Homestead at Point Loma.[33] Despite such beginnings, the authentic phase of the Spanish Revival enjoyed a nationwide vogue following the San Diego Exposition of 1915. The most famous figure in this movement was Bertram Goodhue; the best designer in the medium was George Washington Smith of Santa Barbara.

The bizarre search for a style adaptable to "the Mediterranean blue of our skies and sea, to the mellow brown of our rolling hills in autumn" ended in an attempt to create a domestic vernacular from the architecture of the New Mexican pueblo. This was the dream of the Bostonian A. C. Schweinfurt, who came west with A. Page Brown in the late eighties. Schweinfurt tried the style out on a country hotel near Montalvo in 1894. Somehow convinced that it was "peculiar to this Coast," he attempted at the Hearst Ranch at Pleasanton, and elsewhere, to popularize the adobe walls, projecting end beams, and terraced roofs of the southwest Indians.[34] It was work such as this that moved Frank Lloyd Wright to declare that "the houses in California—Mexican, Hispanic and Hopi—are more atrocious than the skyscrapers of New York."[35]

The development of the California bungalow was one result of the oriental craze growing out of the uncertainty of western propagandists

[33] *Land of Sunshine*, IV (Feb. 1896), 126; Robert Van Norden Hine, *California's Utopian Colonies* (San Marino, 1953), p. 43.

[34] *CA&BN*, XV (Apr. 1894), 39; XX (Sept. 1899), pls.

[35] As quoted in *Architect and Engineer*, CVII (Oct. 1931), 82.

and designers as to what constituted the state's colonial heritage. Although there are those who insist that the redwood bungalow was conceived independently of previous custom and precedent, this architectural form, like everything else in nineteenth-century California, was
imported. The term itself is derived from an Anglicized version of the
word "Bengali" and refers to the thatched houses that evolved from the
Indian service tent used by colonial and military administrators in the
British East. The characteristics that made the bungalow practical in
India and Ceylon, maximum circulation of air achieved by means of
raised foundations and wide verandas, assured its success in California.
Exactly when the bungalow first appeared on the West Coast is less
easily determined than its origin. But as early as November 1888 the
California Architect and Building News published a design by A. W.
Putnam that may well be the progenitor of the redwood bungalow. The
"rustic" wooden house of five rooms with oriental accents had a marked
informality in the arrangement of living space in relationship to the out-
of-doors. Two years after the publication of the Putnam designs, Louis
Sullivan visited San Diego, and upon his return to the East designed two
bungalows for construction at Ocean Park on the shore of Biloxi Bay—
perhaps the first of this architectural species east of the Sierra.

Early in the twentieth century the *California Architect and Engineer*
noted that the bungalow, "as it flourishes in the balmy air of the Pacific
Coast, is just now our especial pride"; a few years later the editors of the
Craftsman praised the "good, simple, straightforward houses" of the
California architects as "closer to the Craftsman idea than any other."[36]
Though the flowering of the bungalow style in California as represented
in the work of the Greenes, Bernard Maybeck, Myron Hunt, and Ed-
gar Matthews belongs to the period after the disappearance of the frontier, it deserves mention here as an unconscious synthesis of the entire
course of California domestic architecture in the nineteenth century. Indeed, the redwood bungalow developed by Charles Sumner Greene
and Henry Mather Greene represents a compromise between the
Spanish-Mexican adobe culture, the New England timber tradition,

[36] *Architect and Engineer*, VI (Aug. 1906), 31; *Craftsman*, XVII (Mar.
1910), 692.

and certain Richardsonian and oriental influences used widely in the West after the Philadelphia Centennial. Thus it is the first indigenous domestic architecture in California.

Charles Keeler, friend of Maybeck and chief propagandist for the Bay Area redwood house, spoke for the bungalow designer when he wrote that the controlling thought in house building should be simplicity and genuineness.[37] Twenty-five years earlier Harold Mitchell and his fellow revolutionists proclaimed an identical sentiment. Their solution, however, was the traditional blind alley of revivalism and led only to failure in the mission movement. In the best of the redwood bungalows there is little of that fatal striving after the picturesque or historic that made the Mission Revival an architectural farce. The bungalow was designed for modern living, and only rarely, as in the use of large boulders in foundations and chimney breasts, was a false element of rusticity introduced. The bungalow plan was open and informal; typically there was a porch across the front and occasionally a patio at the back or garden side. The construction was of board-and-batten or shingles, and the interior was finished in natural redwood. But all of this belongs to the future. It was not until 1903 that the Greene brothers designed a "California house" in Pasadena for Arturo Bandini that combined in one design the adobe builder's talent for site planning and out-of-door living, the clapboard and shingle construction of the New Englanders, and the weathered wood- and stonework of the best of the shingle style.

Although the young men who gathered around Willis Polk and A. Page Brown in the last decade and a half of the nineteenth century considered themselves revolutionists, they were no less colonials than the Franciscans who carried a Spanish edition of Vitruvius with them to the New World, or the architects of the great immigration who reinforced a well-established wood building tradition with the pattern books of Downing and Cleaveland. They were also wrong in assuming that their Early American houses and neoclassic office buildings introduced a new element to California's architectural frontier. For fifty years earlier Thomas Larkin and Walter Colton established the classic tradition in

[37] *Architect and Engineer*, II (Oct. 1905), 27.

western architecture. An immigrant society is always culturally conser-vative. In the century between the mission builders and the Mission Re-vivalists all who built in California were immigrants, and the architec-ture they produced was of necessity colonial.

It was said earlier that the transformation of the American Colonial Revival into the mission movement marked the disappearance of Cali-fornia's architectural frontier. This is true even though the mission craze developed out of an imported eastern revival and was itself a material and aesthetic failure. In acknowledging that they had an architectural past, the Californians unconsciously accepted the fact that the frontier was gone. For until the end of the nineteenth century each successive wave of immigrants brought their past with them and created out of it a colonial architecture sufficient to their present needs. When this frontier architecture in turn became Californian, reflecting regional rather than alien traditions, the frontier phase was clearly ended.

PLATES

1. Mission San Carlos Borromeo, Carmel, 1793. Photograph taken before restoration. Courtesy of the Bancroft Library.

2. House at Fort Ross, 1812. Eugène Duflot de Mofras, *Exploration du territoire de l'Orégon, des Californies et de la Mer Vermeille* (Paris, 1844), I, facing p. 385. Courtesy of the Houghton Library.

3. Casa de Soto, Monterey, ca. 1820. Donald R. Hannaford and Revel Edwards, *Spanish Colonial or Adobe Architecture of California, 1800-1850* (New York, 1931), p. 61. Courtesy of the Architectural Book Publishing Company, Inc., New York.

4. Larkin House, Monterey, 1835-1837. Courtesy of the Bancroft Library.

5. Vallejo Adobe, Petaluma, 1834-1844. Courtesy of the Historic American Buildings Survey.

6. Castro Adobe, San Juan Bautista, 1838. Courtesy of the Historic American Buildings Survey.

7. Colton Hall, Monterey, 1847. Photograph taken before restoration. Courtesy of the Bancroft Library.

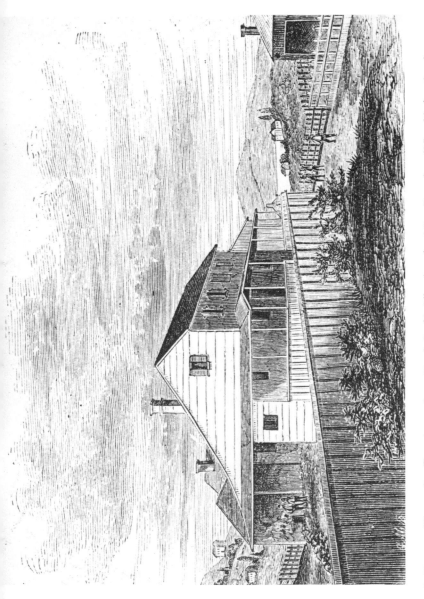

8. Brannan House, San Francisco, 1847. Frank Soulé, *The Annals of San Francisco* (New York, 1855), p. 347.

9. George Perkins Cabin, 1849. Reconstructed for the California Midwinter Fair, San Francisco, 1894. *California Midwinter International Exposition* (San Francisco, 1894).

10. Placerville, 1850. Owen Cochran Coy, *Pictorial History of California* (Berkeley, 1925), No. 172.

11. Niantic Hotel, San Francisco, 1850. Francis Samuel Marryat, *Mountains and Molehills* (New York, 1855), p. 48.

12. Mission Dolores and Parish House, San Francisco, ca. 1850. Courtesy of the Bancroft Library.

13. House, Angels Camp, ca. 1850. Courtesy of the Historic American Buildings Survey.

14. Shurtleff House, Shasta, 1851. Courtesy of the Historic American Buildings Survey.

15. Jenny Lind Theater (Old City Hall), San Francisco, 1851. Union Hotel at right, 1853. At left El Dorado, 1851. G. R. Fardon, *San Francisco Album* (San Francisco, 1856), 7.

16. Methodist-Episcopal Church, San Francisco, 1852. Far right is the Powell Street School. G. R. Fardon, photographer. Courtesy of the Bancroft Library.

17. Humphrey House, San Francisco, 1852. Courtesy of the Historic American Buildings Survey.

18. Montgomery Block, San Francisco, 1853. Gordon P. Cummings, architect. G. R. Fardon, *San Francisco Album* (San Francisco, 1856), 15.

19. Wright's Bank Building, San Francisco, 1854. Peter Portois, architect. G. R. Fardon, *San Francisco Album* (San Francisco, 1856), 11.

20. First Congregational Church, Sacramento, 1854. Albion Sweetser, architect. Courtesy of the Bancroft Library.

21. South Park, San Francisco, 1854. G. R. Fardon, *San Francisco Album* (San Francisco, 1856), 23.

22. Industrial Buildings, San Francisco, 1854. Courtesy of Francis Farquhar.

23. United States Customhouse and Post Office, San Francisco, 1855. Gridley Bryant, architect. Courtesy of the Bancroft Library.

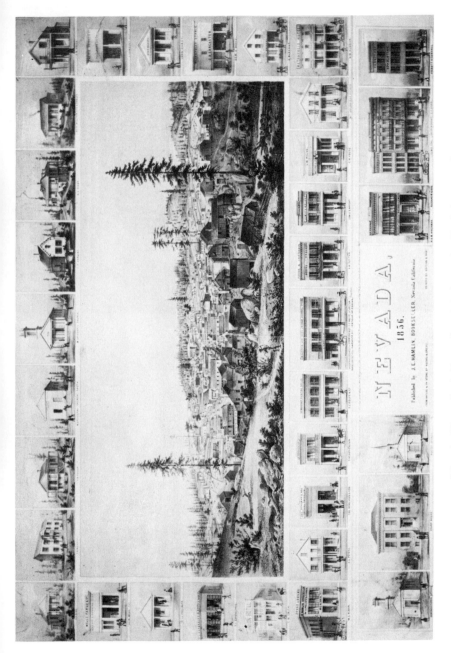

24. Nevada City, 1856. From the original print by Kuchel & Dresel.

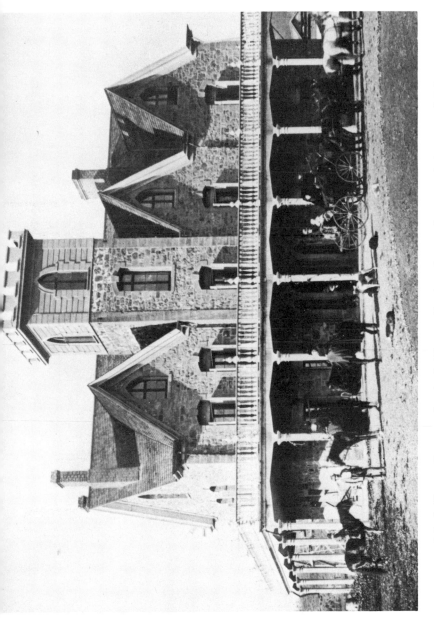

25. Marsh House, Brentwood, 1856. Thomas Boyd, architect. Courtesy of the Bancroft Library.

26. Hibernia Society and Bank Building, San Francisco, 1857. Peter Portois, architect. *Architectural Record*, XX (July 1906), 22.

27. Globe Hotel, San Francisco, 1857. Victor Hoffman, architect. *Architectural Record*, XX (July 1906), 20.

28. Stanford Mansion, Sacramento, 1858. Seth Babson, architect. *California Farmer and Journal of Useful Sciences* (San Francisco), July 4, 1862, p. 1.

29. Westport, Mendocino County, ca. 1860. Courtesy of the Historic American Buildings Survey.

30. Murphys School, Calaveras County, 1860. Courtesy of the Historic American Buildings Survey.

31. State Capitol, Sacramento, 1861–1874. William Ladd Willis, *History of Sacramento County, California* (Los Angeles, 1913), facing p. [5].

32. West End Hotel, San Francisco, 1863. Peter Portois, architect. Courtesy of the Bancroft Library.

33. Banning Mansion, Wilmington, 1864. Courtesy of the Historical Society of Southern California.

34. Bidwell Mansion, Chico, 1865-1867. Henry W. Cleaveland, architect. Courtesy of the Bancroft Library.

35. Temple Emanu-El, San Francisco, 1865-1866. William Patton, architect. Courtesy of the Bancroft Library.

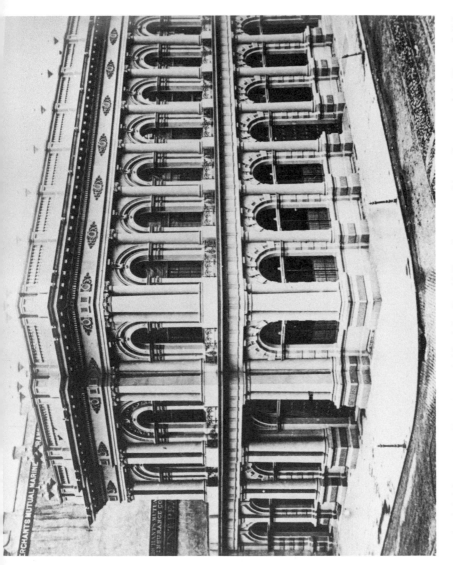

36. Bank of California, San Francisco, 1866-1867. David Farquharson, architect. Courtesy of the Bancroft Library.

37. Banquet Hall, Lick House, San Francisco, ca. 1862. Kenitzer & Farquharson, architects. Courtesy of the Bancroft Library.

38. Pico House, Los Angeles, 1869. Keysor & Morgan, architects. W. W. Robinson, *Panorama: A Picture History of Southern California* (Los Angeles, 1953), Sec. IV, 27. Courtesy of the Title Insurance and Trust Company, Los Angeles.

39. United States Branch Mint, San Francisco, 1869-1874. Alfred B. Mullett, architect. Courtesy of the Bancroft Library.

40. Dibblee House, Ross Valley, ca. 1870. Courtesy of Harrison Dibblee, Jr.

41. Palace Hotel, San Francisco, 1873-1874. John P. Gaynor, architect. Oscar Lewis and Carroll D. Hall, *Bonanza Inn* (New York, 1939), facing p. 20.

42. Palace Hotel, San Francisco, 1873-1874. John P. Gaynor, architect. Courtesy of the Bancroft Library.

43. Fresno County Courthouse, Fresno, 1874-1875. A. W. Burrell, architect. Courtesy of the Bancroft Library.

44. Baldwin Hotel, San Francisco, 1877. John Remer, architect. Courtesy of the Bancroft Library.

45. Flood House, Menlo Park, 1879. Laver, Curlett and Lenzen, architects. Philip W. Alexander, *History of San Mateo County* (Burlingame, Calif., 1916), facing p. 81.

46. Chinatown, San Francisco, ca. 1880. Courtesy of the Bancroft Library.

47. Alcazar Theater, San Francisco, ca. 1880. William Patton, architect. Courtesy of the Bancroft Library.

48. Design for an Eastlake Cottage, 1881. John C. Pelton, Jr., architect. John C. Pelton, Jr., *Cheap Dwellings* (San Francisco, 1882), p. 44.

49. San Francisco Row Houses, ca. 1885. Josef Muench, *San Francisco Bay Cities* (New York, 1947), p. 71.

EUREKA.

Samuel & Jos. C. Newsom
Architects
504 Kearny St
Top Floor
San Francisco.
Cal.

FRONT ELEVATION

50. Carson House, Eureka, 1885. Samuel and Joseph Newsom, architects. Samuel and Joseph Cather Newsom, *Picturesque California Homes*, No. 2 (San Francisco, n.d.), Pl. [40].

51. Carson House, Eureka, 1885. Samuel and Joseph Newsom, architects. Courtesy of the Department of Architecture, University of California, Berkeley.

52. Banta House, Pasadena, 1886. Eugene Getschell, architect. Huntington Library Collections.

53. Crocker House, San Francisco, 1888. Curlett & Cuthbertson, architects. *California Architect and Building News*, X (June 1889), facing p. 78.

54. Oriel Row, San Francisco, 1889. Absalom J. Barnett, architect. *California Architect and Building News,* X (Sept. 1889).

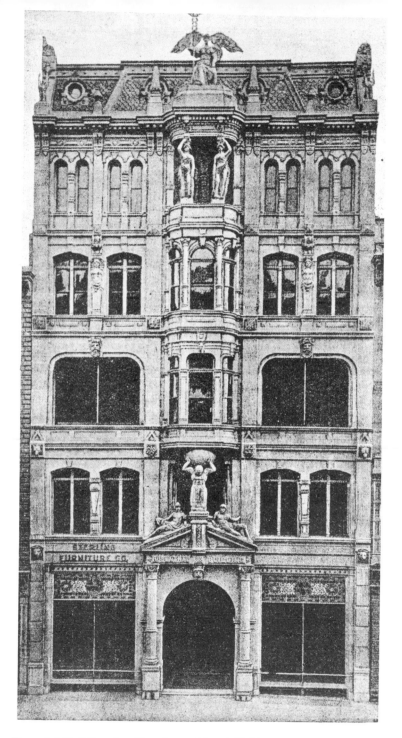

55. Rosenthal Building, San Francisco, 1889. Salfield & Kohlberg, architects. *California Architect and Building News*, X (Sept. 1889).

56. W. B. Bourn Wine Cellar, St. Helena, 1889. Percy & Hamilton, architects. Courtesy of the Bancroft Library.

57. Design for a house by Willis Polk, ca. 1890. *Architectural News*, I (Dec. 1890), Pl. VII.

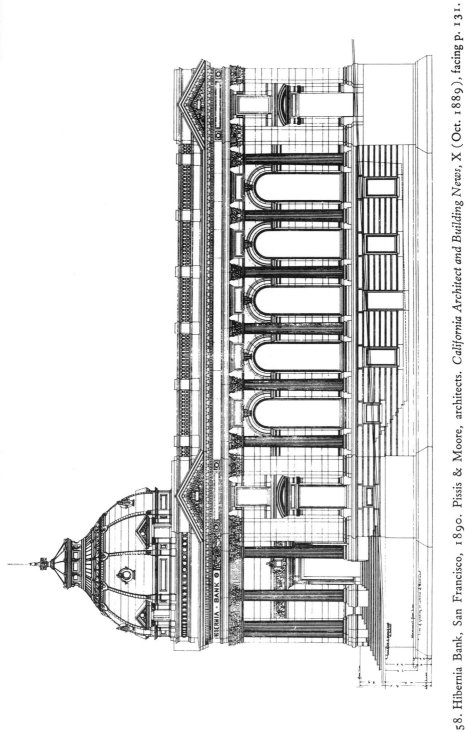

58. Hibernia Bank, San Francisco, 1890. Pissis & Moore, architects. *California Architect and Building News*, X (Oct. 1889), facing p. 131.

59. California State Bank, Sacramento, 1890. Curlett & Cuthbertson, architects.
California Architect and Building News, XI (Aug. 1890).

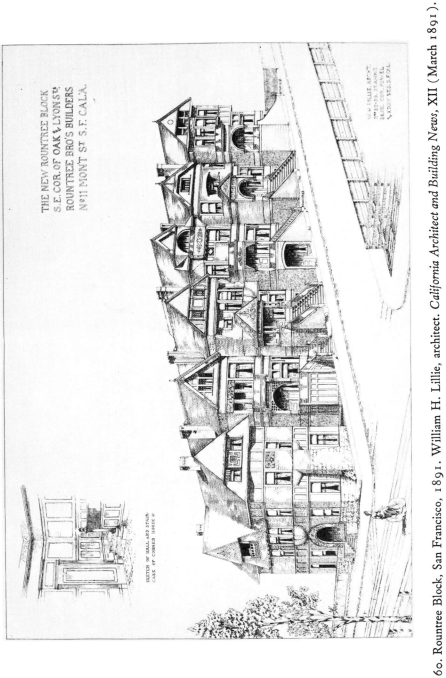

THE NEW ROUNTREE BLOCK
S.E. COR. OF OAK & LYONS ST.
ROUNTREE BRO'S BUILDERS
N°11 MONT ST S.F. CALA.

SKETCH OF HALL AND STAIR
CASE OF CORNER HOUSE &

60. Rountree Block, San Francisco, 1891. William H. Lillie, architect. *California Architect and Building News*, XII (March 1891).

61. Golden Gate Park Lodge, San Francisco, 1896. Edward R. Swain, architect. *California Architect and Building News*, XVII (June 1896).

62. W. B. Bourn House, San Francisco, 1897. Willis Polk, architect. Courtesy of F. Bourn Hayne.

63. Mein House, Oakland, 1897. William Mooser, architect. *California Architect and Building News*, XVIII (Dec. 1897).

64. Examiner Building, San Francisco, 1898. A. C. Schweinfurt, architect. Courtesy of the Bancroft Library.

BIBLIOGRAPHICAL NOTES

THERE is no contemporary bibliography of the materials relating to California's social history. The standard work is still Robert Ernest Cowan's *A Bibliography of the History of California and the Pacific West, 1510-1906* (San Francisco, 1914), of which an expanded second edition was issued in 1933. The best short general discussion of available works is the forty-page "A Commentary on Californiana" in John Walton Caughey's *California* (New York, 1954).

The card catalogues of the Bancroft Library of the University of California, the State Library at Sacramento, the Henry E. Huntington Library and Art Gallery at San Marino, and the California Historical Society in San Francisco, furnish an introduction to the materials available for a study of California architecture. The embryo catalogue of specific architects and buildings at the library of the Department of Architecture, University of California at Berkeley, will in time be of great value to the researcher. The name index at the California Historical Society and the newspaper file at the State Library, although incomplete, serve as a useful indication of what is available.

I. PHYSICAL REMAINS

IN THE study of an architectural frontier there is no satisfactory substitute for the buildings themselves. It is particularly unfortunate, therefore, that the perishable nature of the materials used in California construction, the recurring fires, and the unprecedented growth of the cities have permitted the survival of so little of the work discussed in this book. Nothing remains of the buildings of the gold-rush era, and such well-publicized towns as Columbia represent not the days of '49 but the stage of permanent quartz mining that followed the exhaustion of the placers in 1853. The great San Francisco fire of 1906 destroyed every historic building east of Van Ness Avenue except the Montgomery Block and the United States Branch Mint, and of these the former was razed in 1959 and the latter is presently threatened by redevelopment schemes. The development of the Los Angeles Civic Center and the downtown freeways has left little of the old city other than several highly restored adobes, the Pico House, and the Bradbury Building. More survives in the inland areas, but again these nineteenth-century remains are

197

fast disappearing in the wake of new building, road improvements, and the press of population. Monterey, retaining as it does a relatively large number of restored structures from the period prior to American annexation, is the single important exception to the general poverty of architectural remains from the last century. The major structures that have survived to the time of this writing are noted in the text and footnotes; the best guides to the location of these buildings are the three volumes of Hero Eugene and Ethel Grace Rensch and Mildred Hoover, *Historic Spots in California* (Stanford, 1932-1937), and the Federal Writers' Project city and county handbooks.

II. PICTORIAL SOURCES

PAINTINGS, drawings, lithographs, and photographs are the chief tools for a study of California's architectural frontier. The finest single sources are the Kuchel and Dresel lithographs of California towns, executed between 1855 and 1858, and G. R. Fardon's photographs of San Francisco in 1856. Fifty of the Kuchel and Dresel prints were published by John Howell in Douglas Sloane Watson's *California in the Fifties* (San Francisco, 1936); others are included in Harry Twyford Peters' *California on Stone* (Garden City, N.Y., 1935), which is the authority for lithographic materials relative to the state. The Fardon photographs were first published in 1856 as a *San Francisco Album,* and one of the few copies to be found in California is located at the Huntington Library. Several sets have been reproduced and may be seen at the Bancroft Library and the California Historical Society. One of the few authentic studies of the adobes is a series of paintings executed between 1898 and 1930 by Eva Scott Fényes, housed in the Southwest Museum at Los Angeles. Some of these water colors have been reproduced in *Thirty-Two Adobe Houses of Old California* (Los Angeles, 1950). Other important sources for photographs and prints are the M. H. De Young Memorial Museum and the Wells Fargo Bank in San Francisco. Of the materials scattered in private collections, bookstores, attics, and family albums, there is little present knowledge. The United States Government Printing Office has prepared a partial catalogue of the photographs taken by the Historic American Buildings Survey, and many hundreds of reproductions from this survey pertaining to California are available in the Bancroft Library. About one hundred photographs of surviving nineteenth-century dwellings illustrate Oscar Lewis' *Here Lived the Californians* (New York, 1957), the text of which, unfortunately, is marred by numerous inaccuracies. In some instances the drawings and specifications of nineteenth-century buildings have been preserved. The original sketch for Parrott's Block is in the

California Historical Society, which also possesses some drawings of Henry William Cleaveland; the Society of California Pioneers has the original drawings of the Palace Hotel; Willis Polk's famous design for a peristyle for the San Francisco Ferry Building is at the library of the Department of Architecture, University of California at Berkeley.

III. MANUSCRIPTS

EXCEPT the scrapbooks of Willis Polk deposited with the Department of Architecture at the University of California, there is surprisingly little known manuscript material germane to a study of California's architectural frontier. A few of the letters of Henry William Cleaveland are preserved in the Bancroft and California Historical Society collections, and the author is in possession of some memorandums and letters from descendants of pioneer architects. Many of the manuscripts prepared by the Federal Writers' Project, later known as the Writers' Program, have been incorporated into city or state guides, such as the material on Monterey adobes included in *Monterey Peninsula* (Stanford, 1941). Some pedestrian studies, such as those of George Tays on the Montgomery Block and Colton Hall, are in the Bancroft Library. Perhaps the most important single manuscript is the approximately three-thousand-page study by G. W. Hendry and J. N. Bowman known as "Spanish and Mexican Adobe and Other Buildings in the Nine San Francisco Bay Counties, 1776 to about 1850," which gives complete and accurate descriptions of about eight hundred adobe structures. This work is bound in nine volumes in the Bancroft Library.

IV. HISTORIES

HUBERT HOWE BANCROFT's *History of California* (7 vols., San Francisco, 1884-1890) remains the outstanding single regional monument in terms of scope and materials. It has, however, not inaccurately been called "an immense drifting miscellany," and as a source for the architectural historian it is disappointing. The descriptions of buildings tend to be mere tabulations, and neither Bancroft nor his researchers seem to have recognized that architects have names and histories. The *History of California* (5 vols., New York, 1915), edited by Zoeth Skinner Eldredge, contains a chapter on art and architecture by the San Francisco sculptor, Bruce Porter; a less important short discussion on architecture is included in *A History of the New California* (2 vols., New York, 1905), edited by Leigh Hadley Irvine. Both John Shertzer Hittell's *The Resources of California* (San Francisco, 1863) and Titus Fey Cronise's *The Natural Wealth of California* (San Francisco, 1868) are useful for comments on the influence of red-wood, asphalt, and the Chicago balloon-frame construction on regional building traditions. The recently published *Biographical Dictionary of American Architects* (Los Angeles, 1956) by Henry F. and Elsie Rathburn Withey will be valuable to the California historian when a second edition corrects its multiple errors and inexplicable omissions. Of the many county histories, those published by the Lewis Company of Chicago, such as *The Bay of San Francisco. . . . A History* (2 vols., Chicago, 1892), provide a principal source for brief biographies of the individual architects; those of Smith and Elliott of Oakland, containing hundreds of lithographs of the farmhouses of prominent subscribers, furnish a mine of information regarding rural architecture in the 1870's and 1880's. Two valuable city histories are Frederic Hall's *The History of San José* (San Francisco, 1871) and John S. Hittell's *History of the City of San Francisco* (San Francisco, 1878). *The Annals of San Francisco* (New York, 1855) by Frank Soulé gives much reliable data on gold-rush urban building, such as dates of construction, prices of materials, and labor costs. Most of the important libraries have copies of the various city and county directories that began publication after 1850, many of which contain lists of practicing architects as well as information about public and religious buildings.

V. TRAVEL ACCOUNTS AND REMINISCENCES

THESE ARE among the most valuable sources that the social historian possesses for California architecture before 1853. The best descriptions of pre-gold-rush buildings are in Richard Henry Dana's *Two Years before the Mast* (New York, 1841) and Edwin Bryant's *What I Saw in California* (New York, 1848); a less accurate authority is *Reminiscences of a Ranger* (Santa Barbara, 1927) by Horace Bell. There is a tremendous body of gold-rush writings, most of which is briefly noted by Carl Irving Wheat in *Books of the California Gold Rush* (San Francisco, 1949). The best architectural reporters were the English artists J. D. Borthwick (*Three Years in California* [London, 1857]) and Francis Samuel Marryat (*Mountains and Molehills* [New York, 1855]); Bayard Taylor's *Eldorado* (2 vols., New York, 1850) covers much territory, and Daniel B. Woods's *Sixteen Months at the Gold Diggings* (New York, 1851) contains the best single description of the architecture of the mining regions. *Sixty Years in Southern California, 1853-1913* (New York, 1916) by Harris Newmark and *Sixty Years in California* (San Francisco, 1889) by William Heath Davis are pertinent to both business and building activities in the southern counties in the last half of the nineteenth century. Because of its excellent descriptions of the Chinese settlements and of San Jose, William Henry Bishop's *Old Mexico and Her Lost Provinces* (New York, 1883) is one of the few travel books of the later period important to a study of California architecture. *Over Land and Sea* (London, 1875) by Arthur G. Guillemard and *Lights and Shades in San Francisco* (San Francisco, 1876) by Benjamin E. Lloyd contain references to some of the public buildings and the great hotels of the seventies.

VI. SECONDARY WORKS

THOUGH THE largest body of materials available to the architectural historian falls within this category, there are no secondary works that deal significantly with any phase of frontier California architecture other than mission and adobe buildings. Within this restricted area, the materials vary enormously in worth from such careful studies as Helen Smith Giffen's *Casas and Courtyards: Historic Adobe Houses of California* (Oakland, 1955) to the romantic legends of Lucia Shepardson's *Monterey Roads* (Monterey, 1935). *Ark of Empire: San Francisco's Montgomery Block* (Garden City, N.Y., 1951) by Idwal Jones, though supposedly about San Francisco's Montgomery Block, tells almost nothing regarding this building in an architectural sense; Clarence C. Cullimore's *Santa Barbara Adobes* (Santa Barbara?, 1948), if happily illustrated, lacks any kind of documentation. A better source for the adobes is *Spanish Colonial or Adobe Architecture of California, 1800-1850* (New York, 1931) by D. R. Hannaford and R. Edwards. Marion Randall Parsons' *Old California Houses* (Berkeley, 1952) does not pretend to be a history but is rather a series of tales to accompany the author's impressionistic paintings of picturesque structures. The pamphlet *Southern California Architecture, 1769-1956* (New York, 1956), prepared for the 1956 National Convention of the American Institute of Architects at Los Angeles by Douglas Honnold, is devoted almost entirely to contemporary architecture. Susanna Bryant Dakin's *The Lives of William Hartnell* (Stanford, 1949) is helpful for its discussion of the adobe schoolhouse erected by Hartnell near Monterey, and George Dunlap Lyman's *Ralston's Ring: California Plunders the Comstock Lode* (New York, 1937) contains some references to the building activities of the greatest patron of regional architecture in the frontier period.

VII. MAGAZINES

THE MONTHLY *California Architect and Building News* began publication in January 1880 and ran through the rest of the century. There is no known complete file of this single California professional journal, but most of the numbers are in the library of the Department of Architecture, University of California at Berkeley, and others are available at the State Library, Los Angeles Public Library, and the Library of the University of California at Los Angeles. A second contemporary source is the *Architectural News*, a monthly that was published in San Francisco for only three numbers from November 1890 until January 1891. The only known file of the *News* is at the library at Berkeley. There are several important articles in the national magazines, such at Agnes Foster Buchanan's "Some Early Business Buildings of San Francisco," *Architectural Record*, XX (July 1906), 15-32, and Lyle F. Perusse's beginnings of a study of the Gothic Revival in California in the *Journal of the Society of Architectural Historians*, XVI (Oct. 1955), 15-22. Some of the early numbers of the *Craftsman* contain articles significant to California, such as that on the work of Bernard Maybeck and the Greene brothers in a pictorial study of domestic architecture by Una Nipson Hopkins in Volume XIII (1907-1908), 450-457. Articles of interest on this subject occasionally appear in the publications of the local historical societies. Examples of these are Robert J. Parker's "Building the Larkin House," California Historical Society, *The Quarterly*, XVI (Dec. 1937), 321-335, and Marion Parks's "In Pursuit of Vanished Days," Historical Society of Southern California, *Annual Publications*, XIV (1928-1929), 7-64, 135-207.

VIII. NEWSPAPERS

NEWSPAPERS prove to be generally a disappointing source for factual material on California's architectural frontier. The most important single publication of this nature is the *Alta California*, a San Francisco daily which began printing in January 1849 and continued until June 1891. The infrequent references in the *Alta* to architects and buildings, however, are always brief and often inaccurate. The San Francisco *Call* and the San Francisco *Chronicle* are sometimes valuable for obituaries of individual architects. Newspaper files can be found in most of the large libraries; the State Library has an extensive name catalogue; and the California Historical Society has a number of scrapbooks of newspaper clippings, which are sometimes indexed.

BIOGRAPHICAL SOURCES

CALIFORNIA ARCHITECTS
IN THE NINETEENTH CENTURY

The periodical *California Architect and Building News* cited as *CA&BN*.

APEL, JOHN (-1890). Germany. Arrived 1849.
Crocker-Langley San Francisco Directory, 1868 (San Francisco, 1868), p. 71; San Francisco *Chronicle*, Jan. 15, 1890, p. 3.

ARMITAGE, WILLIAM HENRY (1861-). Sheffield, England. Arrived 1883.
Cosmopolitan Publishing Co., *The Industries of San Francisco, California* (San Francisco, 1889), pp. 154-155; *The Builders of a Great City* (San Francisco, 1891), pp. 105-106; *The Bay of San Francisco*, I (Chicago, 1892), 639.

AUSTIN, JOHN C. W. (1870-). Oxfordshire, England. Arrived about 1892.
Who's Who in the Pacific Southwest (Los Angeles, 1913), p. 19; John Steven McGroarty, *Los Angeles from the Mountains to the Sea*, III (Chicago, 1921), 747-748; *Who's Who in Los Angeles County*, 1950-51 (Los Angeles, 1950), p. 167.

BABSON, SETH (-1907). Maine. Arrived 1850.
Colville's Sacramento Directory, 1856 (Sacramento, 1856), p. 5; Sacramento *Daily Union*, May 21, 23, 1860; *Crocker-Langley San Francisco Directory*, 1877 (San Francisco, 1877), p. 109; *The Bay of San Francisco*, II (Chicago, 1892), 139; San Francisco *Call*, July 15, 1907.

BARBER, PETER J. (1830-). Portage County, Ohio. Arrived 1852.
CA&BN, V (Sept. 1884), 165.

BARNETT, ABSALOM J. (1853-). St. Louis, Missouri. Arrived 1874.
CA&BN, VII (May 1886), 79; X (Sept. 1889), souvenir ed., unnumbered pp.

BENNETT, ALBERT A. (1825-1890). New York. Arrived 1849.
Colville's Sacramento Directory, 1854-55 (Sacramento, 1854), p. 22; *Crocker-Langley San Francisco Directory*, 1877 (San Francisco,

1877), p. 131; Thompson & West, *History of Sacramento County, California* (Oakland, 1880), p. 87; *CA&BN*, V (June 1884), 105.

BENTON, ARTHUR B. (1858-1927). Peoria, Illinois. Arrived about 1887.
Men of California (San Francisco, 1901), p. 426; *Out West*, XXX (Apr. 1909), 321; *Who's Who in the Pacific Southwest* (Los Angeles, 1913), p. 38; James Miller Guinn, *A History of California and an Extended History of Los Angeles and Environs*, III (Los Angeles, 1915), 827-828; *History of San Bernardino and Riverside Counties*, ed. John Brown, Jr., and James Boyd, III (Madison, 1922), 1400-1403; *Architect and Engineer*, XCI (Oct. 1927), 108.

BLACKMAN, HARRY. Poland. Arrived 1886.
An Illustrated History of Los Angeles County, California (Chicago, 1889), p. 384.

BONES, JOHN W. (1818-1901). Valley Forge, Pennsylvania. Arrived 1850.
A Memorial and Biographical History of the Counties of Fresno, Tulare, and Kern, California (Chicago, 1892?), pp. 594-595; San Francisco *Evening Post*, July 31, 1901.

BORDWELL, GEORGE A. (1850-1900). New York. Arrived 1855.
Crocker-Langley San Francisco Directory, 1863 (San Francisco, 1863), p. 73; San Francisco *Call*, Apr. 29, 1900, p. 25.

BOYD, THOMAS. Boston, Massachusetts. Arrived about 1852.
Le Count and Strong's San Francisco Directory, 1854 (San Francisco, 1854), p. 28; *Alta California*, June 12, 1857.

BROWN, ARTHUR PAGE (1860-1896). New York. Arrived 1888.
CA&BN, XVII (Jan. 1896), 1; San Francisco *Call*, Jan. 22, 1896, p. 5; Charles Moore, *The Life and Times of Charles Follen McKim* (Boston, 1929), p. 327; Henry F. and Elsie Rathburn Withey, *Biographical Dictionary of American Architects* (Los Angeles, 1956), p. 79.

BRYAN, ANDREW JACKSON (1848-1921). Missouri. Arrived 1870.
John Albury Bryan, *Missouri's Contribution to American Architecture* (St. Louis, 1928), p. 51.

BUCHANAN, C. W. (1852-1921). Indiana. Arrived about 1889.
An Illustrated History of Los Angeles County, California (Chicago, 1889), p. 385; *Architect and Engineer*, XII (Feb. 1908), 38 ff.

BUGBEE, SAMUEL CHARLES (1812-1877). New Brunswick, Canada. Arrived 1854.
Crocker-Langley San Francisco Directory, 1863 (San Francisco, 1863), p. 84; Frederic Hall, *The History of San José* (San Francisco, 1871), p. 326; *Alta California*, Sept. 3, 1877; June 5, 1878; Shuck papers, California Historical Society.

BUTLER, MINER FREDERIC (1826-1871). Georgia. Arrived 1849.
Charles P. Kimball, *San Francisco Directory*, 1850 (San Francisco, 1870), p. 21; *Colville's Sacramento Directory*, 1857 (Sacramento, 1857), p. 15; *Alta California*, Aug. 24, 1871.

CEBRIAN, JOHN C. See JOSEPH E. MOLERA

CLARK, JOHN J. (1853-   ). New York, New York. Arrived 1858.
Crocker-Langley San Francisco Directory, 1885 (San Francisco, 1885), p. 320; *The Bay of San Francisco*, I (Chicago, 1892), 638-639.

CLARK, REUBEN (1814-1866). Maine. Arrived 1849.
Charles P. Kimball, *San Francisco Directory*, 1850 (San Francisco, 1870), p. 27; *Weekly Alta California*, Aug. 25, 1860; *Alta California*, July 7, 1866; Thompson & West, *History of Sacramento County, California* (Oakland, 1880), p. 92; Sacramento *Bee*, June 17, 1950.

CLEAVELAND, HENRY WILLIAM (1827-   ). Newburyport, Massachusetts. Arrived 1850.
Henry William Cleaveland, *Village and Farm Cottages* (New York, 1856); *Crocker-Langley San Francisco Directory*, 1868 (San Francisco, 1868), p. 142; consult papers in Bancroft Library and California Historical Society.

CORLETT, WILLIAM H. (1856-1937). Isle of Man, England. Arrived 1874.
A Memorial and Biographical History of Northern California (Chicago, 1891), pp. 747-748; *Architect and Engineer*, CXXXI (Nov. 1937), 51.

COXHEAD, ERNEST (1863-1933). Sussex, England. Arrived 1886.
An Illustrated History of Los Angeles County, California (Chicago, 1889), p. 725; *Crocker-Langley San Francisco Directory*, 1890 (San Francisco, 1890), p. 349; *Craftsman*, III (Feb. 1902), pls.; *American Art Annual*, XXI (1924-25), 384; *Pacific Coast Architect* [now *California Arts and Architecture*], XXX (1926), 53; *Architect and Engineer*, CXIII (Apr. 1933), 57.

CRAIN (E), WILLIAM. England. Arrived 1849.
Charles P. Kimball, *San Francisco Directory*, 1850 (San Francisco, 1870), p. 32.

CUMMINGS, GORDON PARKER (1827-1904). New York. Arrived about 1850.
San Francisco Directory, 1852-53 (San Francisco: James M. Parker, 1852), p. 64; *Alta California*, Aug. 2, 1865; Dec. 18, 1869; Feb. 21, 1870; June 25, 1874; Mar. 26, 1876; San Francisco *Chronicle*, Aug. 30, 1904; Idwal Jones, *Ark of Empire: San Francisco's Montgomery Block* (Garden City, N.Y., 1951), p. 59.

CURLETT, WILLIAM (1846-1914). Warrenpoint, Ireland. Arrived 1871.
Crocker-Langley San Francisco Directory, 1875 (San Francisco, 1875), p. 222; *CA&BN*, V (Jan. 1884), 11; VII (May 1886), 80; XI (Jan. 1890), 12; *Who's Who in the Pacific Southwest* (Los Angeles, 1913), p. 110; *Architect and Engineer*, XXXVI (Feb. 1914), 79.

CURTIS, JOHN M. (1852-   ). Warsaw, Illinois. Arrived 1874.
CA&BN, V (May 1884), 91; X (Sept. 1889), souvenir ed., unnumbered pp.; XII (Jan. 1891), Pl. 2; *Crocker-Langley San Francisco Directory*, 1885 (San Francisco, 1885), p. 371; *The Builders of a Great City* (San Francisco, 1891), pp. 127-128; *The Bay of San Francisco*, II (Chicago, 1892), 122-123.

CUTHBERTSON, WALTER J. (1850-1925). London, England. Arrived about 1860.
Crocker-Langley San Francisco Directory, 1881 (San Francisco, 1881), p. 275; *CA&BN*, XIV (Mar. 1893), 30; *Architect and Engineer*, LXXXIII (Nov. 1925), 108.

DAVIS, CHARLES W. (1826-   ). Newburyport, Massachusetts. Arrived 1849.
An Illustrated History of Los Angeles County, California (Chicago, 1889), p. 730.

DAVIS, JACOB Z. (-1896). Pennsylvania. Arrived about 1850.
Colville's Sacramento Directory, 1856 (Sacramento, 1856), p. 38; San Francisco *Call*, Oct. 29, 1896.

DAY, CLINTON (1847-1916). Brooklyn, New York. Arrived 1855.
CA&BN, III (May 1882), 78; III (July 1882), 106; mentioned in letter of David Farquharson to Henry W. Cleaveland, San Francisco,

Oct. 9, 1888, California Historical Society; Ellis A. Davis, *Davis' Commercial Encyclopedia of the Pacific Southwest* (Berkeley, 1911), p. 169.

DEPIERRE, EMILE (1844-   ). France. Arrived about 1870.
Crocker-Langley San Francisco Directory, 1885 (San Francisco, 1885), p. 393; *The Bay of San Francisco*, II (Chicago, 1892), 334.

DORN, FREDERICK R. (1866-   ). Port Henry, New York. Arrived 1886.
James Miller Guinn, *Historical and Biographical Record of Los Angeles and Vicinity* (Chicago, 1901), pp. 631-632; John Steven McGroarty, *Los Angeles from the Mountains to the Sea*, III (Chicago, 1921), 874.

EISEN, AUGUSTUS F. (-1876?). Sweden. Arrived 1854.
Le Count and Strong's San Francisco Directory, 1854 (San Francisco, 1854), p. 50.

EISEN, THEODORE A. (1852-1924). Cincinnati, Ohio. Arrived 1854.
Crocker-Langley San Francisco Directory, 1877 (San Francisco, 1877), p. 303; *Architect and Engineer*, LXXVII (Apr. 1924), 118; William Andrew Spalding, *History and Reminiscences of Los Angeles City and County, California*, III (Los Angeles, 1931), 213-214; see also Augustus F. Eisen.

ENGLAND, THOMAS (1823?-1869). Ireland. Arrived about 1850.
Le Count and Strong's San Francisco Directory, 1854 (San Francisco, 1854), p. 51; Card Index, California Historical Society.

FARQUHARSON, DAVID (-1914). Scotland. Arrived 1850.
Colville's Sacramento Directory, 1854-55 (Sacramento, 1854), p. 39; *Crocker-Langley San Francisco Directory*, 1864 (San Francisco, 1864), p. 153; *Alta California*, Aug. 16, 1879; *Architect and Engineer*, XXXVIII (Aug. 1914), 115; Barber and Baker, *Sacramento Illustrated* (Sacramento, 1950), p. 83; Correspondence, California Historical Society.

GAYNOR, JOHN P. Probably born in New York. Arrived about 1863.
Crocker-Langley San Francisco Directory, 1864 (San Francisco, 1864), p. 171; Card Index, California Historical Society.

GEILFUSS, HENRY (1850-   ). Germany. Arrived 1876.
Crocker-Langley San Francisco Directory, 1879 (San Francisco, 1879), p. 353; *CA&BN*, X (Sept. 1889), souvenir ed., unnumbered pp.; *The Bay of San Francisco*, I (Chicago, 1892), 532.

GOODELL, NATHANIEL DUDLEY (1814-   ). Belchertown, Massachusetts. Arrived 1849.
Robert E. Draper, *Sacramento Directory*, 1869 (Sacramento, 1869),
p. 82; Thompson & West, *History of Sacramento County, California*
(Oakland, 1880), p. 87; *CA&BN*, III (May 1882), 78; *An Illustrated History of Sacramento County, California* (Chicago, 1890), pp.
270-271.

✕ GOODRICH, LEVI (1822-1887). New York, New York. Arrived 1849.
Frederic Hall, *The History of San José* (San Francisco, 1871), pp.
241, 326-327; *Pen Pictures from the Garden of the World*, ed. Horace
S. Foote (Chicago, 1888), pp. 225-227; James Miller Guinn, *History
of the State of California and Biographical Record of Coast Counties,
California* (Chicago, 1904), pp. 297-298.

GOUSTIAUX, G. MORIN (1859-   ). France. Arrived 1869?
David de Pénanrun, *Les architectes élèves de l'Ecole des Beaux-Arts*,
2nd ed. by E. Delaire (Paris, 1907), p. 354.

HAMILTON, F. F. (1851-   ). Addison, Maine. Arrived 1875.
Crocker-Langley San Francisco Directory, 1881 (San Francisco,
1881), p. 430; *CA&BN*, X (Sept. 1889), souvenir ed., unnumbered
pp.

HATFIELD, SAMUEL (1841-   ). Nova Scotia. Arrived 1875.
Crocker-Langley San Francisco Directory, 1889 (San Francisco,
1889), p. 538; *The Bay of San Francisco*, II (Chicago, 1892), 456-
457.

HAVENS, CHARLES I. (1849-1916). New York. Arrived 1856.
Crocker-Langley San Francisco Directory, 1889 (San Francisco,
1889), p. 640; *CA&BN*, X (Sept. 1889), souvenir ed., unnumbered
pp.; *Architect and Engineer*, XLV (May 1916), 109.

HENRIKSEN, BERNHARDT E. (1851-   ). San Francisco.
Crocker-Langley San Francisco Directory, 1880 (San Francisco,
1880), p. 434; *CA&BN*, V (Apr. 1884), 69.

✕ HOFFMAN, VICTOR. Arrived about 1850.
Le Count and Strong's San Francisco Directory, 1854 (San Francisco,
1854), p. 20½; *Architectural Record*, XX (July 1906), 27-28.

✕ HOWARD, JOHN GALEN (1864-1931). Chelmsford, Massachusetts. Arrived about 1892.
Crocker-Langley San Francisco Directory, 1893 (San Francisco,

1893), p. 1530; *The National Cyclopædia of American Biography*, XIV (New York, 1917), 183; *Architect and Engineer*, CXII (Jan. 1933), 48.

HUERNE, PROSPER (1820-1892). Chartres, France. Arrived 1850.
CA&BN, V (Aug. 1884), 147; XIII (Oct. 1892), 111; Daniel Lévy, *Les Français en Californie* (San Francisco, 1884), pp. 163, 173, 184; *The Bay of San Francisco*, II (Chicago, 1892), 452-453.

HUNT, SUMNER P. (1865-1938). Brooklyn, New York. Arrived 1889.
Who's Who in the Pacific Southwest (Los Angeles, 1913), p. 188; *Press Reference Library* (Western Ed.) (New York, 1913-15), I, 66; II, 596; *Who's Who in California*, 1928-29 (San Francisco, 1929), p. 221; *Architect and Engineer*, CXXXV (Dec. 1938), 57.

HYATT, CALEB. New York. Arrived about 1859.
Crocker-Langley San Francisco Directory, 1860 (San Francisco, 1860), p. 174; *Great Register of the City and County of San Francisco* (San Francisco, 1873), p. 203.

JOHNSTON, THOMAS J. (-1875). Arrived about 1860.
Crocker-Langley San Francisco Directory, 1864 (San Francisco, 1864), p. 222.

KENITZER, CHARLES W. (1836-   ). Germany. Arrived 1862.
The Bay of San Francisco, II (Chicago, 1892), 151; *Crocker-Langley San Francisco Directory*, 1893 (San Francisco, 1893), p. 809.

KENITZER, HENRY (1827-   ). Saxony, Germany. Arrived 1854.
The Bay of San Francisco, II (Chicago, 1892), 341-342.

KEYSOR, EZRA F. Arrived 1860.
H. J. Bidleman, *Sacramento Directory*, 1861-62 (Sacramento, 1861), p. 71; Harris Newmark, *Sixty Years in Southern California, 1853-1913* (New York, 1916), pp. 466, 470; Henry F. and Elsie Rathburn Withey, *Biographical Dictionary of American Architects* (Los Angeles, 1956), p. 356.

KOHLBERG, HERMANN (1855-   ). Germany. Arrived 1883.
Crocker-Langley San Francisco Directory, 1889 (San Francisco, 1889), p. 755; *CA&BN*, X (Sept. 1889), souvenir ed., unnumbered pp.

KOLLOFRATH, EDMUND (1853-   ). Baden, Germany. Arrived 1883.
Ellis A. Davis, *Davis' Commercial Encyclopedia of the Pacific Southwest* (Berkeley, 1911), p. 178.

KRAFFT, JULIUS E. (1855-   ). Stuttgart, Germany. Arrived 1874.
Crocker-Langley San Francisco Directory, 1889 (San Francisco, 1889), p. 777; *The Bay of San Francisco*, II (Chicago, 1892), 117.

KREMPEL, JOHN P. (1861-   ). Kreuznach, Germany. Arrived 1887.
James Miller Guinn, *A History of California and an Extended History of Los Angeles and Environs*, II (Los Angeles, 1915), 237-239; *Who's Who in California*, 1928-29 (San Francisco, 1929), p. 220.

KROONEN, LEO (1857-1937). Amsterdam, Holland. Arrived 1886.
CA&BN, IX (Sept. 1888), 125; *History of San Bernardino and Riverside Counties*, ed. John Brown, Jr., and James Boyd, III (Madison, 1922), 1187-1189; *Architect and Engineer*, CXXXI (Dec. 1937), 58.

KUBACH, C. J. Germany. Arrived 1877.
An Illustrated History of Los Angeles County, California (Chicago, 1889), pp. 529-530.

LAVER, AUGUSTUS (1834-1898). Folkestone, England. Arrived 1870.
Crocker-Langley San Francisco Directory, 1877 (San Francisco, 1877), p. 518; Alonzo Phelps, *Contemporary Biography of California's Representative Men*, II (San Francisco, 1882), 90-92; *CA&BN*, V (Jan. 1884), 9; *Architect and Engineer*, LII (Mar. 1918), 89.

✕ LENZEN, JACOB (1838-1910) and LENZEN, THEODORE (1833-   ). Germany. Arrived 1861.
Frederic Hall, *The History of San José* (San Francisco, 1871), p. 289; *Pen Pictures from the Garden of the World*, ed. Horace S. Foote (Chicago, 1888), pp. 363, 621; James Miller Guinn, *History of the State of California and Biographical Record of Coast Counties, California* (Chicago, 1904), pp. 795, 1020; *Architect and Engineer*, XX (Mar. 1910), 99.

LILLIE, WILLIAM H. (1862-1898). Arrived about 1890.
Crocker-Langley San Francisco Directory, 1893 (San Francisco, 1893), p. 883; *CA&BN*, XVII (Jan. 1896), 10.

LO ROMER, JOHN B. (1844-   ). New York, New York. Arrived 1867.
An Illustrated History of San Joaquin County, California (Chicago, 1890), p. 399.

✕ MCKEE, J. O. (1831-   ). Cromwell, Connecticut. Arrived 1849.
Pen Pictures from the Garden of the World, ed. Horace S. Foote (Chicago, 1888), pp. 519-520.

MACY, HENRY C. (1821-   ). Nantucket Island, Massachusetts. Arrived 1849.
Crocker-Langley San Francisco Directory, 1868 (San Francisco, 1868), p. 358; *CA&BN*, V (Feb. 1884), 29; *The Bay of San Francisco*, II (Chicago, 1892), 149-150.

MAYBECK, BERNARD (1862-1957). New York, New York. Arrived about 1887.
David de Pénanrun, *Les architectes élèves de l'Ecole des Beaux-Arts*, 2nd ed. by E. Delaire (Paris, 1907), p. 344; San Francisco *Call*, June 21, 1923; *Who's Who in California*, 1928-29 (San Francisco, 1929), p. 276; San Francisco *Chronicle*, Oct. 4, 1957.

MITCHELL, HAROLD D. (1854-   ). Manchester, England. Arrived 1870.
Crocker-Langley San Francisco Directory, 1881 (San Francisco, 1881), p. 675; *CA&BN*, V (Mar. 1884), 56.

MOLERA, JOSEPH E. (1847-1932). Catalonia, Spain. Arrived 1875.
Who's Who in California, 1928-29 (San Francisco, 1929), p. 439; *Wasp News Letter*, LIII (Dec. 1931), 80; San Francisco *Chronicle*, Jan. 16, 1932.

MOORE, WILLIAM P. (1847-1902). Liverpool, England. Arrived 1880.
Crocker-Langley San Francisco Directory, 1881 (San Francisco, 1881), p. 683; San Francisco *Chronicle*, Sept. 24, 1902, p. 12.

MOOSER, WILLIAM (1834-1896). Geneva, Switzerland. Arrived 1854.
Crocker-Langley San Francisco Directory, 1860 (San Francisco, 1860), p. 231; *CA&BN*, X (Sept. 1889), souvenir ed., unnumbered pp.; San Francisco *Call*, Nov. 8, 1896, p. 14; Bailey Millard, *History of the San Francisco Bay Region*, II (San Francisco, 1924), 330.

MORGAN, OCTAVIUS (1850-1922). Canterbury, England. Arrived 1874.
An Illustrated History of Los Angeles County, California (Chicago, 1889), pp. 566-567; *The National Cyclopædia of American Biography*, XVI (New York, 1918), 364-365; *Architect and Engineer*, LXIX (Apr. 1922), 110.

NAGLE, GEORGE D. (1820-1891). Germantown, Pennsylvania. Arrived 1849.
William F. Swasey, *Early Days and Men of California* (Oakland, 1891), pp. 385-396.

NEWSOM, JOSEPH CATHER, and NEWSOM, SAMUEL. Canada. Arrived about 1855.
Crocker-Langley San Francisco Directory, 1864 (San Francisco, 1864), p. 303; *CA&BN,* V (June 1884), 114; *Architect and Engineer,* XIV (Sept. 1908), 79.

O'CONNOR, PATRICK J. Liverpool, England. Arrived 1852.
Crocker-Langley San Francisco Directory, 1860 (San Francisco, 1860), p. 243; Sacramento *Daily Union,* May 21, 22, 1860; *The Bay of San Francisco,* I (Chicago, 1892), 656-657.

OUGH, JOSEPH (1841-   ). Canada. Arrived 1869.
Thompson & West, *History of Sacramento County, California* (Oakland, 1880), p. 289; *City and County Directory Including Sacramento City,* 1884-85 (San Francisco, 1884), p. 269.

PATTON, WILLIAM (1821-1899). Sunderland, England. Arrived 1849.
Crocker-Langley San Francisco Directory, 1860 (San Francisco, 1860), p. 249; *The Bay of San Francisco,* I (Chicago, 1892), 422; *CA&BN,* XX (May 1899), 55.

PECK, CHARLES S. (1834-1902). Buffalo, New York. Arrived 1852.
James Miller Guinn, *History of the State of California and Biographical Record of the San Joaquin Valley, California* (Chicago, 1905), pp. 1455-1456; Lilbourne Alsip Winchell, *History of Fresno County and the San Joaquin Valley* (Fresno, 1933), p. 71.

PELTON, JOHN C., JR. Probably born in San Francisco.
Crocker-Langley San Francisco Directory, 1877 (San Francisco, 1877), p. 691.

PERCY, GEORGE W. (1847-1900). Bath, Maine. Arrived 1869.
Crocker-Langley San Francisco Directory, 1877 (San Francisco, 1877), p. 692; *CA&BN,* X (Sept. 1889), souvenir ed., unnumbered pp.; *The Bay of San Francisco,* I (Chicago, 1892), 659.

PISSIS, ALBERT (1852-1914). Guaymas, Mexico. Arrived 1858.
Crocker-Langley San Francisco Directory, 1879 (San Francisco, 1879), p. 708; David de Pénanrun, *Les architectes élèves de l'Ecole des Beaux-Arts,* 2nd ed. by E. Delaire (Paris, 1907), p. 374; Ellis A. Davis, *Davis' Commercial Encyclopedia of the Pacific Southwest* (Berkeley, 1911), p. 162; *Architect and Engineer,* XXXVII (July 1914), 94-95.

POLK, WILLIS (1865-1924). Kentucky. Arrived 1889.
Architectural News (Nov., Dec. 1890), passim; Polk scrapbooks, li-

brary of the Department of Architecture, University of California, Berkeley; F. Bourn Hayne collection, Kentfield, California.

PORTOIS, PETER (1812-1900). Belgium. Arrived 1851.
San Francisco Directory, 1852-53 (San Francisco: James M. Parker, 1852), p. 86; *The Pioneer*, XV (Sept. 1900), 142; *Architectural Record*, XX (July 1906), 28-29.

POWELL, ABRAHAM (1828-   ). Philadelphia, Pennsylvania. Arrived 1849.
William F. Swasey, *Early Days and Men in California* (Oakland, 1891), pp. 321-326; James Miller Guinn, *History of the State of California and Biographical Record of Oakland and Environs*, II (Los Angeles, 1907), 809-811.

RANLETT, W. H.
Le Count and Strong's San Francisco Directory, 1854 (San Francisco, 1854), p. 111.

RAUN, EDWARD T. Arrived 1849.
Crocker-Langley San Francisco Directory, 1868 (San Francisco, 1868), p. 462; *The Bay of San Francisco*, II (Chicago, 1892), 146.

REID, JAMES W. (1851-1943). New Brunswick, Canada. Arrived 1888.
Who's Who in California, 1928-29 (San Francisco, 1929), p. 313; *Architect and Engineer*, CLV (Oct. 1943), 36; *The National Cyclopædia of American Biography*, XXXII (New York, 1945), 199; Henry F. and Elsie Rathburn Withey, *Biographical Dictionary of American Architects* (Los Angeles, 1956), p. 500.

REID, MERRITT (-1932). New Brunswick, Canada. Arrived about 1888.
Ellis A. Davis, *Davis' Commercial Encyclopedia of the Pacific Southwest* (Berkeley, 1911), p. 164; *Architect and Engineer*, CVIII (Feb. 1932), 72; see also James W. Reid.

REMER, JOHN A. Probably born in New York. Arrived about 1875.
Crocker-Langley San Francisco Directory, 1879 (San Francisco, 1879), p. 734.

ROUSSEAU, CHARLES M. (1848-1918). Rotterdam, Holland. Arrived 1886.
Crocker-Langley San Francisco Directory, 1893 (San Francisco, 1893), p. 1212; *The National Cyclopædia of American Biography*, XIX (New York, 1926), 378-379.

SALFIELD, DAVID (1861-   ). Keysboard, Illinois. Arrived 1880.
Crocker-Langley San Francisco Directory, 1886 (San Francisco, 1886), p. 1025; George Tinkham, *History of San Joaquin County, California* (Los Angeles, 1923), pp. 1494-1495.

SANDERS, GEORGE H.
Associated with John Wright.

SCHWEINFURT, A. C. (-1900). Boston, Massachusetts. Arrived about 1890.
Crocker-Langley San Francisco Directory, 1897 (San Francisco, 1897), p. 1536; San Francisco *Call*, Oct. 10, 1900, p. 11.

SEADLER, JAMES (1852-   ). Schaffhausen, Switzerland. Arrived 1876.
City and County Directory Including Sacramento City, 1884-85 (San Francisco, 1884), p. 306; Ellis A. Davis, *Davis' Commercial Encyclopedia of the Pacific Southwest* (Berkeley, 1914), p. 709.

SHEA, FRANK T. (1860-1929). Bloomington, Illinois. Arrived 1867.
Crocker-Langley San Francisco Directory, 1889 (San Francisco, 1889), p. 1181; Ellis A. Davis, *Davis' Commercial Encyclopedia of the Pacific Southwest* (Berkeley, 1911), p. 171; *Architect and Engineer*, XCIX (Oct. 1929), 113.

SNYDER, ALBERT A. (-1892). Virginia. Arrived 1849.
Crocker-Langley San Francisco Directory, 1868 (San Francisco, 1868), p. 514; *The Wave*, VIII (Jan. 23, 1892), 1.

SWAIN, E. R. (-1902).
Crocker-Langley San Francisco Directory, 1881 (San Francisco, 1881), p. 904; San Francisco *Call*, Apr. 11, 1902, p. 13.

SWEETSER, ALBION C. (1819-1910). Kennebec County, Maine. Arrived 1849.
Colville's Sacramento Directory, 1854-55 (Sacramento, 1854), p. 85; Thompson & West, *History of Sacramento County, California* (Oakland, 1880), p. 292; Sacramento *Bee*, Aug. 30, 1910.

TEED, MATTHEW (1828-1904). Exeter, England. Arrived about 1850.
James Miller Guinn, *Historical and Biographical Record of Los Angeles and Vicinity* (Chicago, 1901), pp. 842-843; Southern California Historical Society *Annual Publication* (1904), 177-178.

TOEPKE, WILLIAM H. (1870-   ). San Francisco.
Crocker-Langley San Francisco Directory, 1889 (San Francisco,

1889), p. 1277; *Men Who Made San Francisco* (San Francisco, 191 —?), p. 194.

TOWNSEND, LOUIS R. (1832?-1898). New York. Arrived about 1849.
Le Count and Strong's San Francisco Directory, 1854 (San Francisco, 1854), p. 134; San Francisco *Call*, July 7, 1898, p. 12.

VAN DER NAILLEN, ALBERT (1830-1928). Belgium. Arrived 1874.
Crocker-Langley San Francisco Directory, 1889 (San Francisco, 1889), p. 1297; San Francisco *Chronicle*, May 31, 1903, p. 41; *Who's Who in America*, 1926-27 (Chicago, 1926), pp. 1928-1929.

VOELKEL, GEORGE E. (1848-   ). Courland, Russia. Arrived 1872.
Crocker-Langley San Francisco Directory, 1889 (San Francisco, 1889), p. 1304; *The Bay of San Francisco*, I (Chicago, 1892), 535; *Who's Who in the Pacific Southwest* (Los Angeles, 1913), p. 376.

WACKERBARTH, AUGUST (1859-1931). Hesse, Germany. Arrived 1882.
Who's Who in the Pacific Southwest (Los Angeles, 1913), pp. 376-377; *Press Reference Library* (Western Ed.), I (New York, 1913), 593; *Architect and Engineer*, CIV (Mar. 1931), 96.

WALKER, FRANK (1843-   ). Kincardine, Canada. Arrived 1864.
James Miller Guinn, *A History of California and an Extended History of Los Angeles and Environs*, II (Los Angeles, 1915), 473-474.

WALLS, J. A. Buffalo, New York. Arrived 1882.
Greater Los Angeles and Southern California, ed. Robert Burdette (Chicago, 1910), p. 227.

WEEKS, WILLIAM E. (1866-   ). Prince Edward Island, Canada. Arrived 1886.
Architect and Engineer, IX (June 1907), 43.

WELSH, THOMAS J. (1845-1918). Australia. Arrived about 1853.
Crocker-Langley San Francisco Directory, 1872 (San Francisco, 1872), p. 671; *CA&BN*, V (Feb. 1884), 31; Ellis A. Davis, *Davis' Commercial Encyclopedia of the Pacific Southwest* (Berkeley, 1911). p. 170; *Architect and Engineer*, LV (Oct. 1918), 118.

WILLIAMS, STEPHEN H. (1816-1880). New York, New York. Arrived 1850.
San Francisco Directory, 1852-53 (San Francisco: James M. Parker, 1852), p. 104; *Alta California*, July 16, 1867; undated letter (1955) from Williams' granddaughter, Mrs. Jannopolis, to the author.

WINTERHALTER, WILDRICH (1839-   ). Munich, Germany. Arrived 1866.
Crocker-Langley San Francisco Directory, 1877 (San Francisco, 1877), p. 905; *The Bay of San Francisco*, I (Chicago, 1892), 640.

WOLFE, GEORGE H. (1843-   ). Baltimore, Maryland. Arrived 1851.
Crocker-Langley San Francisco Directory, 1872 (San Francisco, 1872), p. 689; *CA&BN*, V (Feb. 1884), 25; San Francisco *Call*, Dec. 4, 1887.

WOLFE, JAMES E. (1820-1901). Baltimore, Maryland. Arrived 1851.
Crocker-Langley San Francisco Directory, 1864 (San Francisco, 1864), p. 418; *CA&BN*, V (Jan. 1884), 3; San Francisco *Call*, Jan. 9, 1901, p. 3.

WOOD, JAMES (1841-   ). New York, New York. Arrived about 1887.
CA&BN, X (Apr. 1889), 45; *The Bay of San Francisco*, I (Chicago, 1892), 644-645.

WRIGHT, JOHN (1830-1915). Killearn, Scotland. Arrived about 1865.
Crocker-Langley San Francisco Directory, 1868 (San Francisco, 1868), p. 584; *CA&BN*, V (Jan. 1884), 10; *Architect and Engineer*, XLII (Sept. 1915), 110.

WYMAN, GEORGE HERBERT (1860-   ). Dayton, Ohio. Arrived 1891.
Arts and Architecture, LXX (Apr. 1953), 20-21, 42-43.

INDEX